Campfire Reflections

Campfire Reflections

T.J. Conrads

Illustrations
by Andrew Warrington

Grouse Creek Publishing

Copyright © 2005 by T.J. Conrads
Illustrations © Andrew Warrington

First Edition — 2005
ISBN: 1-933570-41-5

Published by
Grouse Creek Publishing
9766 W. Mossy Cup St.
Boise, Idaho 83709

   All rights reserved, including the right to reproduce this book or portions thereof in any form by any means, electronic or mechanical, including photocopying, recording, or by any information storage and retrieval system, without permission in writing from the publisher.
   All inquiries should be addressed to Grouse Creek Publications, 9766 W. Mossy Cup St., Boise, Idaho 83709.

Printed in the United States of America

Library of Congress Catalog Number: 2005931767

*In memory of Monty Moravec,
who left the party without saying goodbye.
I miss you, my friend.*

Other Books by T.J. Conrads

The Traditional Bowhunter's Handbook

Table of Contents

Acknowledgements ix
Preface xi

Small Things

1. Sage Ghosts 3
2. Stingrays And Sunny Days 8
3. The Underrated 14
4. Into The Thornbrush 22

Mostly Tailfeathers

5. First Season 30
6. Mountain Blues 35
7. Blindless Birds 41
8. On The Wing 46

Big Game Adventures

9. Post Season 52
10. Across The River 58
11. The Bowl 64
12. True North Adventure 74
13. Prairie Faith 86
14. The Hair Up There 93
15. Kodiak Special 104
16. Nikabuna Nirvana 111
17. Northern Exposure 119
18. One Day At Mackay 131
19. A Never Ending Journey 137

Ruminations

20. The Professor 146
21. The Right Thing 155
22. A Lost Valley 162
23. Remembering Monty 168

Acknowledgements

Special thanks goes to Andrew Warrington, who provided all the illustrations in this book. Having worked with Andrew for several years now, I feel honored to have his work grace the pages of this volume.

Several photos are also the work of friends: Fred Eichler, page 45; Jerry Gowins, Jr., page 151; and Noelle Naiden, who gave me the picture of Monty Moravec shown on page 176. The rest of the photos are from my personal files.

Preface

Hunting with the bow and arrow is much more than just a hobby; for many of us, it is our life. Not only does bowhunting with such simple, yet effective equipment give the hunted game animal the best opportunity to escape, it also teaches wildlife appreciation, outdoor ethics, humbleness and patience. I can think of no other outdoor endeavor that can do all this, and still be highly enjoyable.

It has been said that to know someone, you only need to share a hunting camp with that person. I have found this adage to be true almost 100% of the time. Many of my closest and deepest relationships have been formed around a warm campfire in the great darkness of the outdoors. Many of the stories in this volume depict these events.

My goal was to encompass the entire gamut of the bowhunting experience in North America, from small game to wing shooting and bowhunting birds, and from bowfishing to bowhunting the big game species of North America...from guided hunts to the all-important—and extremely satisfying—do-it-yourself backpack hunts. To round off these bowhunting experiences, I have included several chapters of philosophical ideals and perspectives that may, hopefully, make you appreciate more of the subtle experiences many of us take for granted while traipsing around the woods with bow in hand.

This is my first collection of written outdoor experiences while chasing game with the bow and arrow, something that I never really thought about doing. However, at some point in a writer's career it becomes evident that his work must stand the test of time, and recording that work in book form is one way of appeasing this self-serving idealism. Some of these essays have appeared in previous editions of *Traditional Bowhunter®* Magazine. I appreciate the opportunity to rework them for inclusion in this volume along with many never before read works. If I have done anything of value here, it will be the success of this combined effort.

T.J. Conrads
Trinidad, Colorado
2005

"I doubt whether any man takes keener enjoyment in the wilderness than he who also keenly enjoys many other sides of life; just as no man can relish books more than some at least of those who also love horse and rifle and winds that blow across lonely plains and through the gorges of the mountains."

Theodore Roosevelt

Small Things

Campfire Reflections ══════════════════ **One**

Sage Ghosts

I love the high desert. The vast expanses of sagebrush and deep canyons of the Snake River Plain have been a large part of my adult life. The endless bowhunting opportunities it provides is astounding. Mule deer, antelope and bighorn sheep, as well as sage grouse, chukar and Hungarian partridge, Valley quail, several species of waterfowl and dove abound in this environment. However, one game animal gets very little recognition, the cottontail rabbit.

Fast, sneaky but very stalkable, the cottontail is a wonderful bowhunting quarry. It lives and thrives in the open sagebrush and can be hunted from September to February in many of the western states, and there are more liberal seasons back east. Not only does the cottontail allow off-season bowhunting action, it is absolutely fabulous on the table. And nothing cures my wintertime cabin fever like escaping into the sagebrush hills and flats with my longbow in hand, and my Lab by my side.

My first experience bowhunting cottontails was many years back when our local archery club used to hold its annual rabbit hunt the last week of February. I can distinctly remember the feeling of accomplishment I had when I finally connected with my first rabbit. It had run through the sage and stopped under one of the aromatic bushes when I ran an HTM rubber blunt clean through it. The excitement of taking the first one led to many other trips into the high desert, usually after all the other bow seasons were over.

While hunting javelina in south Texas a few years ago, I had one of the best rabbit hunts of my life. I had already tagged my first javelina and was interested in shooting a wild hog. My hunting partner, Greg Jouflas, had just arrowed his first javelina and he and another friend were out retrieving it, so I decided to hunt near the lodge for hogs.

Just outside of camp I jumped a cottontail. Then there were three...then ten. There were so many rabbits I had a hard time keeping track of them as they jumped around in the low grass by a water tank. I missed the first three or four, then settled down and brought the next five to bag with five arrows. With all my broadheads dull, and one broken arrow, I headed back with several brace of fresh rabbit on my belt.

Back in camp I started a fire in the bar-b-que pit with some mesquite wood and worked on a recipe while the wood turned to coals. By the time Greg had returned with his javelina, the aroma of fresh rabbit was wafting through camp. As soon as Greg had his javelina hung in the cooler, I had a fresh salad, wine and several tasty rabbits on the table next to the campfire. Dinner in the desert was never so good, and I learned that these small game animals would add tremendously to my enjoyment of hunting with the bow and arrow.

Cottontails, which are of the genus *Sylvilagus*, can be found in almost every state, as well as the southern part of a few Canadian Provinces and most of Mexico. There are four species of rabbits called cottontails, and several others that are in the same group. The most widely distributed species is the Eastern cottontail, *Sylvilagus floridanus*, which can be found in all states east of the Rocky Mountains, as well as all of Mexico and the southern parts of New Mexico and Arizona. The mountain, or Nuttall's cottontail, *Sylvilagus nuttali*, is the second most widely distributed cottontail, and is found on the western slope of the Rockies and into the west coast states. The other species are the desert cottontail, *Sylvilagus auduboni*, which live in the open country from western Texas to the Pacific and north into Montana, North Dakota and California; the pigmy rabbit, *Sylvilagus idahoensis*, which is the smallest of the cottontails and lives in the sagebrush country of the western states; the marsh rabbit, *Sylvilagus palustris*, and the swamp rabbit, *Sylvilagus aquaticus*, which can be found in most of the southern states; and the New England cottontail, *Sylvilagus transitionalis*, which prefers the mountains from northern Alabama through the Appalachians and into the mountains and brushy areas of New England.

Rabbits are prolific breeders, with does cutting loose with up to five or six litters a year, although three to four is more normal. Being cyclical in production, rabbit numbers vary considerably from year to year, although they still offer reasonable hunting even in low production years. Many studies on rabbit reproduction and depredation show that on average 85% of each year's rabbits are killed, whether hunted or not, by many factors, the largest being depredation by predators.

Besides the fantastic hunting cottontails provide, especially for the bowhunter, they are delicious on the table. Adding a few cottontails to the camp larder, or the home kitchen will add tremendously to your dining experience.

What a grand season it had been. On my annual Montana whitetail hunt with my good friend G. Fred Asbell, I was lucky and filled both my antlerless and antlered deer tags. This year Montana had failed to sell all of its nonresident antlerless whitetail tags, so I ran into town and was able to secure two more. This was the year to fill the freezer with tender deer meat.

As fate sometimes happens, the next morning I was hunting deep in a cottonwood swamp when the big ten point buck I had already given up on walked by less than 15 yards away while pushing two does. No buck tag...been there, done that...got the T-shirt. So I waited until the lead doe was ten yards away and sent the cedar shaft down through her spine. She dropped on the spot and started to spin around as I laid another through her heart. It was over in a matter of seconds.

The buck just stood there, unable to comprehend what had just happened. Another, bigger doe came running up from behind the buck to see what all the commotion was and I slipped her a 4-blade Zwickey Delta through the top of the lungs. Still, the buck just stood there and I grimaced at the fact that my greediness to fill my buck tag with a much smaller buck had left me looking at one of the largest whitetail deer I had ever seen.

With all my tags filled, I was relegated as camp cook and driver while Fred and the rest of the gang continued to hunt. It was a strange feeling to not have anything to hunt for two days, and I was just about feeling sorry for myself when I saw a rabbit hop out from an old homestead from across the gravel road from the cabin. I grabbed my bow and a few Zwickey Judos and headed out after it.

The first arrow was low and the cottontail jumped and ran into the low scrub near the homestead. I scanned through the sage and honeysuckle, but the rabbit seemed to have disappeared. A slight movement caught my eye as the rabbit hopped into another bush. A well-placed Judo and I had the makings of dinner. An hour later, three rabbits were lying on the porch. What had turned into the end of the deer hunt now had me hunting the scrub brush and cottonwoods for the wily cottontail. By the end of the hunt I had added a few more rabbits and had spent several wonderful hours stalking, shooting and, yes, missing these little speed demons.

The chukar hunting was rather bleak and I was working my way back down the hill when a rabbit scurried across the two-track I was descending. Since I usually have a bow with me, I stopped at the truck and traded the over and under Citori for my longbow and loaded up my quiver with a series of Judos and rubber blunts. I hadn't gone ten yards into the sage when a cottontail bolted from between my feet. Leading the rabbit, I loosed the Judo only to see it fall several feet behind the fleet-footed creature.

I retrieved the arrow and just stood there looking into the sagebrush around me. I knew the rabbit hadn't gone far. Then a glitter of reflected light caught my eye and as I studied the spot a pair of ears materialized. Slowly I nocked, came to full draw and picked a spot. At the shot I knew I had the little devil. As I went to retrieve my prize, all I found was a clean shaft; the little beast had slipped away into the sage like a ghost.

Molly, my Lab, was sniffing down the rabbit's scent when it bolted from her and ran straight down the trail we were on. Without much thought the arrow was away. Imagine my surprise when the Judo and rabbit met with a resounding thud, the two tumbling over and over with Molly fast on the trail. As the dog handed the rabbit over to me—arrow half way through as well—another cottontail scurried by. I placed the dead rabbit in my game strap on my belt and we were off for more high desert adventure.

By late afternoon we had six rabbits to show for our work; not a bad day by any means. Hot, tired and thirsty, both Molly and I made our way back to the truck for some much needed hydration. We sat in the cool shade of the truck as the sun set over a glorious silhouette of Idaho's southern Owyhee Mountains, the dog nuzzling the small, furry rabbits as I looked forward to the delicious meal they would provide when we returned home.

Once again, the high desert had surprised me with a bounty that was almost forgotten, and once again I came to appreciate what these little sage ghosts provide, not only in bowhunting excitement, but in culinary delights as well.

Two ================================ *T.J. Conrads*

Stingrays and Sunny Days

The early morning sun's rays glittered across the open water as the boat slowly motored along the shallows of the bay. The sweet smell of salty water combined with the wave action and sounds of sea birds mesmerized me as I closed my eyes and dreamed of far off places and times gone by. Caught up in the moment, I heard Rob's voice boom through the light breeze and the hum of the small outboard.

"Ray off the starboard bow!"

I quickly glanced right just in time to see the vague shadow of a cownose stingray dart past the boat, followed by the sweet sound of a loosed bowstring, and the splash of a heavy fiberglass arrow as it slipped beneath the sea's surface only to glide effortlessly behind the ray. Scott Taylor, a friend I hadn't seen much of in twenty years, had missed his first ray of the day.

I turned my attention back to the sea and tried to soak in the warmth of the summer sun and the pleasure of the moment. Born in the tropics, I have always loved being in and around the ocean, and right now all I wanted to do was enjoy the feeling of being on the water again. Besides, there was still plenty of time for hunting stingrays. I knew the rest of the day and the morrow would bring some of the most fantastic bowfishing I had ever had, and time to re-acquaint myself with a long lost friend, and with the ocean.

Earlier that spring I was invited to speak to the Traditional Bowhunters of Maryland in Baltimore. Before I flew out, I remembered an old friend I had worked with over two decades earlier. He had divorced, moved back to Maryland, and remarried. I remembered he also used to bowhunt, so I made a few inquiries, found his number, and made contact. Plans were made to get together in Baltimore, talk some bowhunting, and spend some time getting caught up on all the years.

During the course of the two days I was in Baltimore, club member Rob Davis invited Scott and me to come out and hunt stingrays with him on Chincoteague Bay. I have arrowed plenty of carp and other rough fish over the years, but the offer to come and possibly shoot a 100-pound stingray was just too much. I made the decision right then and there to come out in June.

"Just bring your bows. I have all the gear. You can stay with me," Rob said as we parted after the banquet.

Scott picked me up at the airport the following June and we headed down to Salisbury, Maryland, where Rob lives in a beautiful log home on a large track of timber. He and his wife Betty Lou were gracious hosts, making us feel at home while there. After dinner we shot a few rounds in Rob's backyard 3-D range, discussed our gear and plans for the next day, and retired for the evening.

Rob uses a bowfishing system he developed over several decades for taking big stingrays as well as lemon and brown sharks. A 16 to 32 ounce plastic pop bottle sprayed inside with florescent orange paint, and then expanding foam, is attached to a fish arrow with about 20 feet of 400 pound test Dacron string. The string is wound around the bottle and slipped under a wire flipper that has been attached to the bottle with an old bicycle inner tube. This keeps the string taut and out of the way while drawing the bow to shoot. A rubber cup—the type used on the bottom of a folding steel chair leg—is mounted to the bow with a bolt via the accessory insert. Since my longbow doesn't have such an insert, I used Great Northern's Traditional Gadget Adapter. This little beauty works wonderfully for attaching any fishing gear to a traditional bow, and I have used it on several occasions while bowfishing. The top of the bottle is then slipped into the cup where it is held with enough friction that it stays snug. The idea is that when a hit has been made, the string will pay out as the fish takes off. When the string gets to the end, the bottle pulls out of the rubber cup. It is at this point you must follow the floating orange bottle until you can get another arrow into the fish and start to bring it to bag. Trying to land large stingrays with a fixed reel or bowfishing spool is a good way to lose your entire setup. Rob's system allows the arrow and bottle to escape the bow when a large ray is hit.

Our plan was simple: motor the boat slowly through the shallows until we saw a ray; point the tip of the arrow at the ray once spotted; Rob would motor in the direction the arrow was pointed; then either Scott or I would shoot the ray. Well, that's the way it's supposed to work, but getting the feel for shooting at fast moving cownose stingrays was a challenge, as was hitting the slower, but much larger, southern rays that swam at deeper depths.

Our self-imposed limit was no more than ten rays a day. Now all we had to do was find them.

The next shot opportunity was mine and when the swift cownose ray darted by I was able to strike it in the right fin. The line paid out, the bottle blasted from the bow, and the chase was on. Rob motored up to the bottle and I pulled in our first ray of the day.

The cownose is a lovely stingray, if lovely is an accurate word to describe such a beast. But as with the huge manta ray—a stingray that can exceed 20 feet in length—the cownose has a much more graceful appearance than other rays. And its speed and agility in the water make it an ideal quarry with the bow. Its tail is a thin, wire-like affair, much like a piece of thick cord or a strong twig, with the ever-dangerous stinger at the base of the tail.

The southern stingray is much bigger, with a fleshy tail and more rounded appearance. There are records of southern stingrays weighing well over 150 pounds, and Rob has an award system for anyone he takes out: shoot a stingray over 100 pounds, and he gives you a unique and original T-shirt that depicts all the stingrays that reside on the East coast. My plan was get one of those shirts, but Rob reminded me he has only given away six shirts in all the years he has been taking people bowfishing. Obviously, I had my work cut out for me.

Southern stingrays have a large set of crushing plates in their mouths for breaking up clams and other bivalves, one of their main food sources. While sitting on the bottom of the bay, they suck large volumes of mud and water through their gills, siphoning it away until a clam is found. Then they use these crushers to break the hard shells and eat the clam. Often times you will see small, muddy circles where they are feeding. By slowly moving over the murky water you can catch a glimpse of the ray and, hopefully, get an arrow after it.

Stingrays get their name from a stinger that is connected to the body near the base of the tail. The stinger is actually a modified dorsal fin. Some rays will have double and even triple sets of stingers. They grow right on top of each other and each stinger is unique in shape and size. The stinger is a defense mechanism that is used when the ray is attacked. It is a hard, bony growth that is serrated like a knife with barbs that point back, and covered with a mucus slime. When attacked, the stingray will whip its body back and forth, its tail flying all over as it tries to hit its enemy. When contact is made—and I might add that in the case of southern rays this force will knock a grown man down—the stinger is thrust into the attacker and easily pulls away from the stingray. The result is an excruciating pain, and in the case of humans the possibility of infection if not removed and the wound cleaned immediately. Rob showed me photos of the result of a battle he had with a southern ray that placed a stinger completely through his sneaker and foot. The message sunk in quite well, I might add, that by all means I needed to stay away from the tail until the stinger has been removed.

We continued to motor around the bay and soon came upon what looked like a brown circle lying on the bottom of the ocean floor not ten feet below the boat. It was about three feet in diameter and while I was trying to figure out exactly what it was, Scott let loose with an arrow. When his arrow hit the object, all hell broke loose.

At the impact, the round, dark object took off like a bat out of hell, literally. Line whizzed off Scott's bow...the bottle blasted off into the sky like a rocket. I looked at Scott and his eyes widened.

"Whoa! That was cool!" was all he said.

I looked back into the bay and all was quiet except for the wake where the bottle had entered the water some 30 odd yards away from the boat. It was gone...along with the stingray. We sat there for several minutes, glassing all over the bay...nothing. About five minutes later, several hundred yards away, I saw the orange bottle zipping across the water. The chase was on. Rob fired up the boat and poured on the gas, only to have the engine die before we had closed in half way to the now disappearing bottle.

Fortunately, after about ten minutes, Rob got the engine started. But this would be an event we would endure for two days: the engine would flood and foul the spark plugs. It was an inconvenience, but we would work through it.

As we motored up to the bottle I could see the huge southern ray below the bow of the boat. I drew back my bow and sent a 1500-grain glass shaft into the beast. Now we had two arrows in it and it was only a matter of time before we were pulling it up. When the ray was beside the boat I was amazed at its size: it was just at 70 pounds, one of several huge rays we would shoot.

Common sense dictated the use of the "Bopper," a heavy piece of hickory with a five pound steel ingot on the business end to bring the beast to bay. A couple of bops, a jab of the gaff, and we hauled the ray over the side. First piece of business was to grab the ray by the tail with a leather glove and cut the stinger off. A few rounds of congratulations, several photos, and we were off to find more rays.

The following day was much the same: several stingrays were bagged, we basked in the warm sun, spent hours discussing world events and bowhunting, and cleaned fouled plugs.

By midday we were motoring across the bay heading for another shallow spot near Assateague Island when I noticed a stream of brown water rolling by in front of us. I mentioned this to Rob but he wasn't sure what was causing it so we motored up the milky stream for almost 200 yards until it ended in a huge pod of 20 to 30 southern rays. They were swarming in one area, digging beds in the soft mud of the bay searching out clams. From the looks of things they had found one very large clam bed. It was a fantastic sight to see several rays, most of them over 60 pounds, so Scott and I picked out the biggest one and proceeded to anchor both arrows in the stingray. Once we had it aboard we weighed it in at 83 pounds. This was the largest stingray we took over the two days.

By mid afternoon we had bagged all the rays we could stand and headed to a grassy island to clean them. Stingray meat is a delicacy, and at one time was commercially harvested and served in several local restaurants. But over fishing and government regulations have reduced stingrays to a bowfishing quarry. One ray has several pounds of edible meat. Each wing has a slab of meat on top and bottom, so four chunks of this delicate flesh was removed from each ray. Being an avid proponent of eating what you kill, I had little trouble reducing the boatload of rays into dozens of five to ten pound slabs of meat for taking home.

On the way back the engine finally died. Unfortunately, we were a long way from the shore so the next few hours were spent oaring against the current until the water got shallow enough to get out and pull the boat to shore. By the time we got to the boat ramp the sun had set and we were engulfed in darkness.

Back at Rob's we grilled several pounds of stingray steaks, shared a bottle of wine, and enjoyed the evening. The two days had been relaxing for me, as my hectic schedule of travel every spring usually ends up raising my blood pressure until I just have to escape. This short but exciting break was well deserved and much needed.

On the flight back to Seattle a few days later, I slowly drifted off to sleep with the scintillating images of the eastern sun glistening off the water of Chincoteague Bay, the flashing arrows and darting stingrays, and a time of new and renewed friendships.

I knew I would come back. Besides the fun and camaraderie, I still need to earn one of Rob's special T-shirts.

Three
T.J. Conrads

The Underrated

Wild pigs are probably the most underrated bowhunting animals in the world. Not recognized by either the Boone & Crockett or the Pope & Young Clubs, they have not been given their due when it comes to quality animals to pursue, especially with the bow and arrow. In fact, the wild pig may be the most perfect quarry for the bowhunter.

They are intelligent, cunning and tough, probably one of the toughest game animals to put down even with well-placed broadheads. And they have given me immeasurable hours of pleasure stalking them over three continents, taking me around the world. To top off all this, wild pigs provide some of the finest eating meat you will ever taste, from the lowly feral hog to the Russian boar and African warthog.

My first encounter with a wild pig was in Texas quite a few years back. I had a day to hunt with a friend and we headed off to the scrub land of south Texas to chase the javelina, *Dicotyles tajacu*, which is not really a wild pig, but rather a distinct species unto itself, the family *Tayassuidae*, that it shares with the white-lipped peccary. Even though I didn't shoot one on that trip, it whetted my appetite to start pursuing the wild pigs of the world.

There are seventeen known species of swine in the world today, all under the family *Suidae*. Seven of these live in Africa, which include the warthog, bush pig, Red river bush pig and the giant forest hog. Javelina are not related to any swine alive today, sans their southern cousins, the white-lipped peccary. Their closest relative is an extinct giant hog that roamed the Earth over 25 million years ago. Remains and fossils found in the Agate Springs Quarry in Nebraska of this giant hog reveal it had a skull that measured over three feet in length, quite a comparison to its New World brethren, the javelina, or Collared peccary.

A few years back, my friend Don Thomas wrote about the Ham Slam, a collection of wild pigs from around the world that would lampoon any of the Grand Slams of the day: sheep, deer, caribou or whatever. Don and Ray Stalmaster discussed what species should be included in the so-called Ham Slam and came up with the following; it must contain a javelina from North America, a warthog and bush pig from Africa, and an Old World boar, *Sus scrofa*.

I have given this Ham Slam a lot of thought, and my own personal decision on this unofficial collection of world swine ends up with five species. I figure you have to add the feral hog to any collection since it is the most widely distributed pig in North America. Feral hogs are hybrids, containing Russian boar and domesticated Eurasian pig genes.

Domesticated pigs were first brought to North America in 1539 by the Spanish explorer Hernando de Soto, who released them in Florida. Then in 1893, Austin Corbin imported 50 true Russian boar from

Germany's Black Forest, placing them in his private game preserve in the Blue Mountains of New Hampshire. Then in 1900, twenty Russian boar from Germany were released in New York's Adirondack Mountains. This went on for many years until 1912 when 14 Russian boar—this time actually caught in Russia—were released into a private preserve in the western mountains of North Carolina known as Hooper's Bald. No hunting was allowed on this 600-acre preserve until 1920 when a European-style hunt, using horses and spears, was conducted. During the ensuing melee, hundreds of the boar were able to escape into the countryside where they bred with the domesticated pigs of the de Soto era to become the hybrids we call the feral hog today. In fact, there are no true Russian boar living outside of game preserves in the United States; they are all considered hybrids.

I was hunting in the swamps around the Okmulgee River in southern Georgia with Don and Lori Thomas. We were guests of Cory Mattson and Joey Buchanan at the Paradise Hunt Club. Since one of the greatest pleasures of bowhunting new areas is the encounter with different flora and fauna, I was caught up most of the week photographing the eerie swamps with the gum and cypress trees, draped with Spanish moss, surrounded by the brilliant green of palmetto and leafing hardwoods. It was the most relaxed hunting trip I had ever been on, and I was enjoying myself immensely as I spent each day wandering through the lush Georgia swamps.

We were hunting hogs, with the side offering of possibly running into an Eastern wild turkey, and the hog hunting was living up to its description: tough. I was seeing small sounders each day and was getting stalks, but by the time I worked in close the pigs would be nowhere in sight. It was as if they had a sixth sense and knew the bogeyman was lurking in the woods. Of course, that was me!

One day I asked Joey to drop me off on the far side of the property so I could spend the day hunting back toward camp along an old river road. As I got out of the truck I heard a turkey gobble. Joey grabbed his turkey gear and went after the tom; I headed off down the old road in search of pigs.

The road was grown over with just a path to walk along. It was pleasant to hunt, as it was up on a slight rise with low borrow pits on each side. This little height gave me a good view well into the woods on both sides of the old road. I kept hearing what I thought was a gobble, but cast off the thought knowing Joey was nearby, but the sound kept getting louder and louder as I continued hiking. When I came to a bend in the old road, I dropped my hunting pack and grabbed my turkey reeds, slipping one into my mouth as I moved off about 15 yards into the palmettos.

The swamp was quiet when all of a sudden a booming gobble exploded just over a rise in front of me. I gave a couple of hen purrs and then he appeared, as if by magic. The old tom was strutting for all his worth in the swamp, moving between palmettos and dragging his wings in the water. I had an arrow nocked, but the distance was just too far to take a shot. Another couple of purrs and he stopped, stood straight up and looked right at me. It was bye-bye time. In a flash he bolted and I cackled at him. He stopped, but kept a watchful eye in my direction as he slowly circled around behind me. Within a few minutes he was again gobbling and walking down the middle of the old road I had just left.

Everything was looking good, but I have hunted turkeys with a bow enough to know you cannot take anything for granted. This tom didn't let me down. As he strutted his way closer and closer, his head shot straight up, then he looked straight down, and promptly tore down the river road, putting until I couldn't hear him anymore. Frustrated, I stood up and walked back to where he was when he bolted. There, right in the middle of the road, was my hunting pack.

Tell me turkeys are stupid.

It was a great week. I had seen several sounders of pigs, shot a copperhead snake and a turtle, missed a possum and had a close encounter with an Eastern gobbler, one of the toughest turkeys to bag—with a gun or a bow. But now it was time to get intimate with a wild pig.

I had noticed there was one particular spot on the property where hogs were feeding early in the morning and late in the evening, so I got up into a treestand early in the afternoon where I could watch over a huge section of palmettos and hardwoods. Hours pass slowly in a treestand for me, so before too long I was down on the ground doing what I do best: still-hunting. As I made my way out toward the river and a road that would lead me back to camp, I heard a sounder of pigs moving

through the palmettos. Nocking an arrow, I slowly closed the distance until I saw the first rooter with its head down in the dirt. There were four of them, one being a little bigger than the rest. As they moved past me, I shot the larger pig as it stood behind a palmetto frond. It grunted and ran about 20 yards before it fell. The rest of the sounder just stood around like nothing was wrong until I stood up. After the dust settled, there was only me, my bow, and the dead pig left as the night slowly enveloped the swamp.

Back in camp I got Joey to come and help me load the swamp rooter into the truck. In the beam of the flashlights I took a good look at the pig, running my fingers through its course, dusty hair. I knew right then I would be spending a lot more time hunting pigs the rest of my life.

It is mid January and I am again in the South hunting feral hogs and deer. I am in the company of good friends—Greg Jouflas, Nathan Andersohn, Max Thomas, Andy Carpenter, Billy Ellis and our camp host, Spence Bonjean. We are guests of Toxey Haas at his Lee Haven Hunting Camp in eastern Alabama. Toxey, who designed the Mossy Oak line of hunting camouflage, wants us to have a good time here, and there is no doubt we will.

Campfire Reflections

Everyone has been seeing plenty of game, and Nathan has shot the first deer. With a limit of a buck and doe a day, we are not too worried about getting into the deer. But the hogs have been tough. They always seem to know when you are just about ready to make the last step for a clean shot, or hear your last footstep crack a small branch as you ooze closer. Nathan has never shot a wild pig and he has his sights sets on bagging one. I, on the other hand, have added a few more species since last spring, but would still like nothing better than to take one of these hogs with my new longbow, *Askari*. It is a fine bamboo takedown Dick Robertson made for me, and has lived up to its name. It has become my friend in the hunt.

The first day is fantastic. I pass on an average size buck and see several other deer moving through the fog as it drifts over the swampland. Greg, Billy and I spend the middle of the day chasing rooters through the swamps and forests, never getting a decent shot but loving every minute of it.

That evening I am walking out early from my stand. I can only handle sitting for a few hours before I get bored and start still-hunting through the woods. I come to a field where I am supposed to meet Andy...a little early...and find several pigs rooting around the fringes. Nocking an arrow, I move up to what little brush I can find and look over the field. Pigs are everywhere, maybe 20 to 30 of them, from lone boars to sows to piglets. They are fighting with each other, themselves or the air. It doesn't matter; they are being pigs.

Since I cannot move without being seen, I simply kneel and wait to see what events may unfold. Besides, it is rather interesting watching the antics of this many pigs together. Before long a good size pig darts toward me, growling and grunting. I don't know if I have been spotted, but it certainly seems so. At less than ten yards, the pig turns broadside and stops. My arrow is away before I can think and I hear the telltale sound of a hit. A grunt and a squeal and the field is empty; the pigs have all disappeared into the woods next to me. It is also starting to get dark, so I find a place to sit and wait for Andy.

As I go over the shot again and again in my mind, I am sure I have either double lunged or liver shot the animal. Ten minutes later Andy shows up and tells me he missed a pig twice at the other end of the field. We look for my arrow and find it less than ten yards away, covered with dark red blood. A quick glance with our flashlights verifies only one thing—the pig is hit hard: blood is everywhere in good amounts, all the way into the woods.

The blood trail is heavy, but after 150 yards we hear a grunt and crashing. With the night going to be cold, we decide to bag the trailing until the morning.

Only a hunter knows the true length of night when he has a wounded animal out there in the woods. Even though I was sure of a good hit, I have hunted too many pigs to feel giddy about recovery in the morning. My mind plays games with the movie running through my head until sheer exhaustion takes over and I fall asleep.

Tough, tough animals.

The next morning, less than 20 yards from where we stopped and marked the trail, we find the pig dead.

During the week we shot more deer, a few rabbits, and I took a possum for a full mount in my office. And there was a firefight in the river cane between Greg, me and a little swamp rooter that, despite his lethal wounds, continued to charge us. For my own part, I have to admit I lost three arrows trying to save my buddy in the melee, all the arrows ricocheting off the cane and over into the river. But in the end we got him, and then we ate him for lunch the next day. At 30 pounds, he was, as Spence would say, "a snack hog," and a damn tasty one at that.

Toward the end of the hunt we decided to do a hog drive through a large portion of a swamp. Spread out and laced with florescent orange vests, we slowly worked around until we had come into an impenetrable mass of brambles. Greg and I took the right and Max and Nathan ran the middle. Within 100 yards of the road, a sounder containing several hogs in the 200+ range busted out of the bramble thicket right in front of Greg and me. When we got to where they had crossed, we ran into Nathan. One of the pigs had doubled back and Nathan shot it as it crossed his path.

A few of us started to blood trail while Max took the outside. Within five minutes, Max came across the dead hog on the trail. The arrow had cut straight through the left lung and angled out the liver, and Nathan had his first hog with a bow.

Tough, intelligent and crafty, wild pigs are supreme bowhunting animals that have not been given the respect they deserve. And with the added benefit of bringing something special to the table, it's hard not to look at them from a chef's point of view. The opportunities to hunt wild pigs are many, and growing all the time as they begin to move into new territory and more and more bowhunters find out what a fantastic game animal they make.

As of today, I have collected all five species of the coveted Ham Slam with a longbow. The last species, the bush pig, took me almost 22 days of hard hunting in the Save River jungle in southeast Zimbabwe, where rogue bull elephants kept me in trees several nights and the black mambas roamed during the day. I managed to kill two bush pigs, and plan to go back again some day, but that story will be told later....

Wild pigs deserve a place in every bowhunter's heart. They just may be the most perfect big game animal to pursue with the bow and arrow, and one of the finest eating as well. I certainly think so.

Four — T.J. Conrads

Into The Thornbrush

I remember the first wild pig I ever shot at. It was a javelina, and it was in Texas several years back when I loosed a hurried arrow right over one's back. I'll never forget that shot, or how the javelina sort of materialized out of the Texas brush, and slipped back into it like it was never there.

It was that experience that told me I would have to come and hunt these musk rooters again, but it would be several years before I would have the chance. Now I was back in Texas, about 25 miles from the Mexico border, in some of the most inhospitable country in North America. Everything growing in this part of south Texas has horns or thorns, not to mention ticks and fleas.

The skunky smell of a javelina wafted down the arroyo I was hunting. I turned to my hunting partner Greg Jouflas and with a nod and smile I said, "Javelina." No sooner had the word popped out of my mouth than the pig grunted at us through the brush and bolted.

The sun was pitifully hot that day, and just ratcheted up a few more degrees as we continued on our way.

Javelina, *Dicotyles tajacu*, are not related to any known pigs in the world today. In fact, they are in their own family, *Tayassuidae*, with their closest ancestor a gigantic wild pig that roamed the planet 25 million years ago during the Lower Miocene period. From jaws and teeth found in Agate Springs Quarry in Nebraska, paleontologists have estimated the javelina's closest relative had a skull about three feet in length.

Javelina is the Spanish name given these unusual animals because of their javelin-like tusks, The proper name, *peccary*, is derived from the Brazilian Indian word *pecari*, which literally translates "animal which makes paths through the woods." The collared peccary is the species in the northern part of its range, which includes Mexico, New Mexico, Texas and Arizona. At one time they were distributed as far as Arkansas, but unbridled hunting decimated their ranks.

Besides having the unique physical feature of only one dew claw on their rear hooves, javelina, or musk hogs as they are known throughout much of their range, have a scent gland on their back about six to eight inches up from their short tails. This gland has many uses, not the least of which is having the ability to keep track of each other in the thick brush they call home. This unique feature also allows the hunter to locate them when they are nearby, and with a constant southwest wind, I was using my nose more than my eyes in locating these desert ghosts.

I was hunting the Las Pintas ranch in southwestern Texas with my friend and hunting companion Greg Jouflas. Kent Ostrem of Mahaska Custom Bows had called and told me he had a new ranch with fantastic

hunting and accommodations for the javelina hunter, and since I was interested in hunting these musk hogs once again, I jumped at the opportunity. Besides, March in the Northwest is about as dreary as it gets, and I needed to see some sunshine if I was to keep my sanity.

The first morning was beautiful—cool, clear and crisp as we exited the rental van and started to hunt down Sendero Cinco, our designated hunting area. We had no sooner entered the sendero when we were deluged with cottontail rabbits. They were literally coming out of every cactus and bush. The ensuing firefight brought only one to bag, thanks to Greg, and left a couple of humbled bowhunters standing in the morning breeze.

Half a mile down the sendero the smell of a javelina drifted from the brush to the north. But it was too late. The brush erupted and all was quiet again. By mid-day we had seen only two of these desert dwellers and returned to the van for lunch and water. As we made short conversation on the walk back to the vehicle, Greg bent over and procured something from the ground.

"Well, look at this!" he said as he held out a perfectly shaped arrowhead that looked Paleolithic in shape and design. I glanced down at the ground, then back at the chipped stone in his hand.

"Not a bad find," I muttered as I inspected the head. By the time we got back to the van we had found two more, one of them a more modern game tip chipped in the delta shape. If there were javelina in the hot south Texas sun that day, we never would have known it.

This part of Texas was grassland for thousands of years, turning to thorn tree and cactus after several generations of regular burnings by native peoples and natural events. But some time before that it must have been one heck of a forest. The amount—and size—of petrified trees here is astounding. In the ranch house the fireplace hearths are rimmed with huge petrified trees, as are all the walkways and parking areas.

Back at the ranch, Greg and I took in lunch and a beer on the back patio where we could watch a sendero that runs away from the house. It was cool in the shade of live oaks as we sipped our drinks and talked about the history of this area. But then a small sounder of javelina crossed the sendero within about 200 yards of the house and we were off in hot pursuit.

If you have never hunted the brush country of south Texas, let me explain a little about it. If it were not for the roads, or senderos, cut through this thick maze, you would probably never find javelina, much less a way out. As soon as you step a few feet off a sendero or an arroyo, the brush literally grabs you. It is so thick that in most places you either have to follow cow trails or crawl on hands and knees just to get through. To add insult to injury, let's just say that everything in Texas has horns or thorns! Add a longbow and back quiver and you have the ingredients for a bout of foul language.

An hour later I felt like a cat had had its way with me. The brush had torn my shirt to shreds, and blood ran down my arms and face. The thought of shooting a javelina had escaped me long ago. Right now I wanted to find my way out of the hellish brush.

Then there was the telltale smell, and I looked up just in time to see three musk hogs sneak by in the brush. Even at ten yards, there was no shot. And by the time I got an arrow nocked on my longbow they had simply walked out of sight. If I were going to get a crack at a javelina, I would have to change my hunting tactics.

The next day Greg and I hunted through more open country in another part of the ranch. This pasture was more or less half prickly pear cactus with lots of grass between. It made for great stalking, but after six hours of hunting we only saw the tail end of one javelina.

That afternoon we were back at the ranch house, eating a sandwich and drinking a pop while watching over our newly named Patio Sendero. It was much easier to watch the half-mile road from the patio during the middle of the day while sipping a cool drink, rather than beating the brush in the Texas heat. But being this close to the bunkhouse makes for fast acting nap attacks by early afternoon. I fought the urge, but

Greg succumbed and soon was asleep in his bunk while I kept vigil.

It must have been an hour or so, but I jerked my head up from a nodding spell to see a sounder of javelina crossing the sendero. Grabbing my bow, I leaned into the bunkhouse; Greg was fast asleep, so the stalk was mine. Within 20 minutes I was on an old cow trail that cut through the thick mass of brush the javelina had gone into.

The wind was perfect, but the trail was heading away from where I had last seen the javelina. I found an arroyo, which swept through the brush and dropped into it as I slowed and nocked an arrow. Moving crosswind, I picked up the skunk smell...I was close. Out of nowhere I spotted a lone javelina facing me head-on at less than ten yards. As I slowly raised the bow to shooting position should the little tusker provide its vitals, it turned and whirled as it grunted. Then the brush exploded with javelina, and they were running all around me.

I glanced to my right and saw a single javelina walk past through the grass and right behind another javelina that was looking my way. I led the walking one and shot when it presented itself through an opening. The arrow caught the little musk hog high in the lungs, passing completely through and smacking into the prickly pear cactus behind it. With a grunt, the two of them ran off a short distance and started growling. The air was filled with their musky odor.

Even without much of a blood trail I found the javelina not more than 15 yards from where I had shot it, stone cold dead, in a patch of cactus. As the cool breezes of the late afternoon filtered through the thorn brush, I had to take a minute to admire the little musk hog and this harsh environment it calls home. Up close they seem much bigger, and their salt and pepper coat of bristles seems to fit this harsh place.

I have a firm conviction that as hunters we should eat what we kill. Stories abound around the edibility of javelina, from delicious to "like eating a skunk!" Well, after skinning the tusker I hacked off one hindquarter and both of the back straps and headed toward the mesquite coals flickering in the barbecue pit. The meat looked fine and smelled good, so I flopped it on the grill and basted it with a mixture of Greek spices and tarragon oil. When it was what I considered to be done, I whacked off a chunk and plopped it in my mouth.

It was dry, but edible. Not great, but would make good sausage.

Laughter erupted from the crowd of bowhunters that had gathered at the grill to watch this event. After watching me go for seconds, they all soon took a knife to the javelina and before too long it was all gone.

Another myth refuted.

The next day Greg went off to hunt javelina while I decided to take a swing at the ridiculously high population of cottontails that had started to overwhelm our spread. After a half hour and several lost or broken cedar arrows, I had three brace of bunnies, which I cleaned and slipped over a bed of Mesquite coals just before Greg rolled into camp. He was able to connect on a large javelina deep in the Texas brush. The first arrow had caught the tusker a little low, and when it charged toward him in the brush, Greg was able to slip another arrow down through its back as it raced past him. But that is another story in itself.

The sun was slipping low in the West as we sat down to a dinner of fresh roasted rabbit, salad and a bottle of red wine saved for just such an occasion. We savored the moment, and reminisced about the past week we shared hunting the little desert dweller and promised to come back. As dusk turned to darkness, the sound of the night slowly wafted up through the thorn brush and the moon's glow lit up the land.

Indeed, we would be back.

Mostly Tailfeathers

Five ═══════════════════════════ T.J. Conrads

First Season

Coming To Terms With The Wild Turkey

The offer was too good to ignore: "Why don't you come on out and hunt turkeys with me?" Dick said on the phone. My mind swam for a minute....

"I'll be there!" I found myself blurting into the receiver. I had never hunted these big game birds and now had a reason to do just that. A phone call to my travel agent and I was booked on a flight to Billings, Montana, where Dick would pick me up.

The first morning Dick, his son Yote, and I worked our way down into a steep draw of pine and fir, following the unusual gobble of a tom in the bottom. Now, some people may not find the voice of a gobbler fascinating, but for me it was a first and I was caught up in an ethereal trance, just like the first time I ever heard an elk bugle in the wilderness.

The morning was alive with the sounds and smells of the forest as we worked down a draw on Dick's property. Whitetail deer bounded away quietly through the trees, and songbirds started to sing as we descended into the draw.

"Get behind those trees," Dick whispered. "I'll call from back here and try and bring him in to you." Sounded easy enough, but what was to follow was anything but easy turkey hunting. Dick called, the tom gobbled, and I stood in the shadows for an hour not seeing a bird. Try as he might, Dick just couldn't get the bird to budge from the top of a ridge covered in fir. The old boy had a harem of hens with him and obviously didn't see the need to come down and find one more.

We worked in closer throughout the morning until the tom finally gave us the slip and shut up. After a short regroup, Yote decided he wanted to stalk down the draw toward the last place the tom had gobbled, so Dick and I went the other way.

After another couple hours of unanswered hen clucks, Dick turned to me. "Let's go eat some breakfast," he said. Back up the ridge we went to find the truck. Crossing a fence I looked down and saw a smattering of blood on the grass. As I looked over to Dick, I noticed he was standing there muttering under his breath at the exact spot the truck used to be.

A simple deduction was in order.

"It looks like Yote shot a bird," I said.

"Probably a porcupine!" snapped Dick.

"Then why did he take the truck?"

"Damn kid!"

We walked back toward the house discussing this infraction by his oldest child. A quick look up toward his parents' house revealed where the truck had gone. Within a minute, we saw the truck barreling down the road heading toward us, with dust, weeds and all kind of field fodder flying out from behind it. As the truck came to a skidding stop, Yote was wearing a grin from ear to ear. After the three of us had split up earlier he ran into two toms fighting. As they took turns stomping each other around the woods, Yote stalked within ten yards and slipped a Snuffer through one tom's neck. It put its head down and turned away from the fight, but the other tom kept up its attack until the shot bird dropped to the ground. Satisfied with his show of force, the second tom strutted off over the hill.

As Yote approached the bird it jumped up and looked at him and tried to make a run. But youth served Yote and the battle ended in a hurry. The old tom sported an eight-inch beard. As we listened to Yote's story back at the house, I saw Don Thomas' truck coming down the road. As the dust settled Don opened the back of his truck shell and proudly produced a tom he had shot the evening before. It was more than a turkey hunter could stand, two birds with longbows in one day's time.

Although I have lived relatively close to huntable turkey populations during the last decade or so, I've never taken the time to go out and hunt them. After my first day of turkey hunting with Dick I was hooked. There is something special about being out in the woods after a long, cold winter with a longbow in hand. The purple crocus blossoms and fresh, green shoots of grass are the promise of spring, and they covered the forest floor where I walked.

I spent the next several days with Dick trying to lure a tom within bow range. Hell, I even missed one after spending an hour trying to convince him I was a lovesick hen. Overshooting a turkey at less than ten yards with a longbow is a hard thing to admit, but hey, Dick was right behind me, laughing, so there it is.

After a few days I decided to go over and spend some time with Don hunting turkeys around his place. Besides, Dick needed to turn out some bows and I'm sure if I hadn't left he would have never gotten back to work. Such are friends. Don and I spent several days trying to find a cooperative bird, but it was not to be. After fruitless morning hunts I'd find myself drinking a cup of coffee on Don's porch listening the wind chimes, staring out over the expanse of coulees thinking about the elusive turkey.

As the days wound by I found myself learning more about these strange birds. I finally understood their magnetic qualities that change relatively sane individuals into obsessed creatures of the predawn. Drooping heads and baggy eyes adorn these poor souls every spring, and I'm afraid I have joined this crazy tribe.

It is early October and I am lying on Don's couch reading H.G. Wells' *First Men In The Moon* for the umpteenth time... it is one of my favorite books from my childhood. Montana is experiencing an unusually warm fall, and I am enjoying it as best I can. The sounds of the wind chimes blowing in the breeze make me reflect back to the past spring. It was here I had laid and listened to their soothing tunes, falling asleep in the warm spring weather. Dreams of bronze birds, red snoods and gobbling fools tumbled through my head. And all the while the chimes played a mystical lullaby to me. Funny, I'm back at the exact spot a full five months later doing exactly the same thing. But this time it is a fall bird I'm after, not the cagey bird of springtime.

The first night I am sitting in a treestand overlooking one of Don's barley fields. In my pocket are two tags—one for turkey and one for an antlerless whitetail. Even if the evening should bring nothing more than a sunset I will be happy. Hell, just being out and enjoying the scenery is enough for me. After all, I'm here on holiday.

As I settle into the stand I hear a familiar yelp of a hen turkey. They are there, below me in the coulee. As the sun starts to settle down onto the horizon I catch movement to the south. First there is one, then a flock. Before too long I have counted a group of 26 turkeys feeding out into the field in front of me. They are acting like fools, hopping around and running and jumping and flapping their wings. They look like kids out in a playground, not at all like the wary birds I encountered in the spring.

It has taken an hour before they have approached close enough for me to judge their size. Soon they are overtaking my position and I am having a hard time picking one to shoot at. The situation is a riot; birds are hopping and yelping and acting like idiots, pecking at each other and clucking loudly, and I find myself smiling at their antics. But it is time to make a decision, and I choose to shoot the big tom that is making his way toward me. As he approaches I mentally visualize my arrow taking him squarely in the breast. At the last possible moment he spins and walks away. Caught off guard, I make the decision to shoot him through the back. The arrow is away and looks good, then there is a loud crack and feathers are flying. The ensuing cacophony of beating turkey wings and yelps leaves me in a flustered state. When the dust has settled I see my orange-fletched arrow buried in the dirt surrounded by a half dozen or so tail feathers of the tom. Another clean getaway for the bronze bomber...and another chapter of knowledge has been etched into my personal memory.

In the next few nights I will see the flock again. One evening Don was working his way to a treestand when he came across the turkeys feeding in the field. He slowly oozed them toward me as I sat in a stand over the crest of the field. But as the birds approached the edge of the field they took flight. The sound of a couple dozen turkeys flying through the trees you're hiding in is enough to make you drop your bow, believe me. They careened down the slope, landing in a scattered pattern, and started calling to regroup. As the evening approached I came down from my stand and made my way toward where the birds had alit. I just had to see where they were.

When I came near where I expected them to be, I made a few kee-kee-run calls and was immediately rewarded with a cackle from above. I looked up and saw a large tom bouncing around in the top of a Ponderosa pine. He was a large bird, but I never actually thought of shooting him out of the tree. It just didn't feel right. He quickly got tired of me standing below and he took flight. But there were many birds that flew by me and I called again to find out where they were. A low yelp came from above and I strained to look for the bird. I scanned all the pines around me and couldn't see anything that resembled the size of a turkey. In fact, every tree looked void of anything but thinly placed branches. Then all hell broke loose. Every tree held a bird or two and they all took flight at once. The hair on the back of my neck stood up as it rained pine needles and feathers around me.

It is another pleasant fall afternoon as I sit on Don's porch drinking a beer and listening to the wind chimes blowing in the breeze. Lori, Don's wife, has placed two sets of these wind chimes at different levels of the house and I, for one, am entranced by their tuned tones drifting through the air. They remind me of Montana, turkeys and my friends who live here. The sounds, and the panoramic view from the deck, confirm I am where I should be right now.

It has been a fantastic year getting to know the wild turkey. Tomorrow I will have to head home. Deadlines call me back, and fires need to be put out in the office. But today it is enough to sit and listen, and to recall the bronze bomber for which I came here to meet on its terms.

And that I did.

Campfire Reflections ════════════════════ **Six**

Mountain Blues

It was the last day of deer and elk season in Idaho. My hunting partner, Nick Nydegger, still had an unused elk tag and we had just spent the entire day chasing a bull until he finally gave us the slip late in the afternoon. Calling it a season, we proceeded to pull ourselves up out of a deep canyon that had several old mine shafts and cabins hidden throughout its depths.

As we climbed up a well-used trail toward the rim I spotted a large blue grouse as it jumped up on a log that was across the old miner's trail. The shot was uphill, about 30 yards, and I removed a Judo-tipped shaft and promptly bowled over the bird. As the feathers settled, I could actually taste the rich flavor of the bird after roasting it over an open fire back in camp...a fine way to end the hunting season.

When I walked up to the log the bird was hanging down, its head on the ground, mouth open, and feet sticking up in the air with its eyes closed. My orange-feathered shaft was sticking straight up and as I grabbed it the bird's eyes opened and that damn thing blasted under the log, breaking my arrow off about half way, and rocketed down the hill! The last thing I saw was when it banked a hard right, seemingly going Mach 1, with my shaft hanging out of it.

So much for dinner.

Upset about this incident and feeling the need to devise a new head for killing these large birds, I had the bright idea I needed more shocking power on the business end of my arrows. The next year I armed my shafts with solid steel blunts. These, I knew, were going to be the panacea I needed to kill these blue brutes.

The first morning of the following hunting season I was walking down a trail when I saw a blue grouse sitting on a branch of a large white pine about twenty yards away. With all the confidence in the world, I pulled the steel blunt arrow from my quiver, took careful aim, and loosed the lethal shaft. THHWWAAACKK! I drilled that bird solid and it came rolling out of the tree, feathers floating in the wind, deader than a doornail...or so I thought. At about two feet from the ground the bird locked its wings and rocketed over my head, the orange shaft buried halfway through its body. Again, I watched in complete horror as the grouse flew off into oblivion, with my arrow, both of which were never seen again.

Since that time I always carry a slightly dull 4-blade Zwickey Delta for big grouse and have not lost one since. Oh, I still carry a Judo and have killed several smaller species such as ruffed and forest or spruce grouse, as well as squirrels and rabbits. But for big blues, only a broadhead will do in my book.

Blue grouse are large birds, the largest of the mountain grouse. Their prime habitat is high elevation fir, pine and spruce forests broken up by creeks and small rivulets. Rarely have I found them at low elevations where I hunt. They prefer to stay as high as they can, following the snow line down in the fall and winter, and back up in the spring when the snow slowly melts. At times, I have found them in groups as large as thirty or more birds, all in September, hovering between 9,000 and 10,000 feet.

Table fare of blue grouse can run the gamut from tender, melt-in-your-mouth texture to shoe leather, depending on how old—and how large—the bird is. And it is this size difference that creates a quandary: shooting small, younger birds while bigger, older birds are present is easier said than done...bigger just seems better at these times.

And nothing adds to the evening fireside meal like a fresh grouse. Roasted whole over a fire, as is my preference for a young bird, or baked in a Dutch oven with freshly picked wild mushrooms and a splash of red wine, it is hard to beat a grouse meal in hunting camp.

I classify grouse in one of four personal biased categories, and hunt them accordingly: sitters, roosters, runners, and flyers, the later better known as rocketeers. The first three are huntable with a bow, but for the latter indigents, a scattergun is most appropriate, and I have no problem using one when necessary.

Sitters are what I want. These birds will just sit still and let you shoot them, which is fair game as far as I am concerned when I have a longbow in my hand. Sometimes they jump behind a tree or walk away from you allowing an easy stalk and, sometimes, several shot opportunities.

One season while hunting elk in a lost valley somewhere in central Idaho I came upon a covey of young ruffed grouse. They were feeding in a current bush and I proceeded to shoot every arrow in my quiver, killing four of them with four arrows as they moved through the bush. I resharpened my broadheads, tied the double brace of birds to my hunting pack, and headed down the hill after a bugling bull. Not twenty yards farther, a large spruce grouse walked out from under a pine. A Judo made quick work of him as well and added to the wonderful dinner that night. As for the elk, well, I never saw him that day. But the grouse hunting was fantastic....

Although western spruce, sage and ruffed grouse are more likely to sit and let you smack them where they stand, most blues do not allow you to get very close before they move into the next category: roosters.

Roosters are grouse that flush, usually right in front of you, and land in a nearby tree. Most of these birds can be hunted successfully if you are a good shot. Blues tend to be a little more skittish than western ruffs and spruce grouse, and as you move in close enough for the shot they either start squawking or fidgeting, or they sit there thinking you don't see them. I like the latter ones and this seems to be the way I shoot most of my blues. Of course, you will lose quite a few arrows unless your shot is accurate, and I should know; I have several dozen arrows lying around the woods and forests as proof. In fact, this is probably as good a time as any to admit that I have de-quivered on a roosting grouse more than once…and twice on one bird that lived to tell all its friends about the event. There are still three broadhead-tipped arrows in that tree....

Runners are just that: grouse that would rather run from you than sit or fly away. They can be hunted, but you had better be in good shape to keep up with them. They are adept at using trees, shrubs and rocks to keep screened from your view so your shots will be quick, and usually at a moving target.

Just this past week I ran into a covey of blues—a fleet would be more accurate as there must have been over two dozen of the birds in a large patch of huckleberries. I was returning to camp after a morning deer hunt when a half dozen or so of the largest grouse I had ever seen trotted off through the trees in front of me. At first I thought they were turkeys they were so big. I started after them when all of a sudden the entire flock took off running. I shot and missed the first bird, and then they ran over to the edge of a ravine. They had already run down to the small rivulet and were running up the other bank when I sent a 4-blade Delta through the back of one large specimen. By the time I recovered the flopping grouse, the rest of the covey were already across the ridge and down the other side. I chased those birds for another twenty minutes until they finally disappeared in some thick brush. I counted myself lucky, and then returned to pick up my bird. At least I had dinner.

And then there are the rocketeers, which take flight at the first sign of danger and don't look back. They are like B-52s taking off as they flush with a riot of wing beating and fanfare, and don't stop until they have put considerable distance between you and them. Forget these dudes; you might as well have a shotgun and good retriever rather than a bow in hand.

The year had been busy. Moving and setting up a new office had taken most of September, which is my local deer and elk bow season. After deciding the office could live without me for a few days, I packed up the truck and made my way to the hills of one of my favorite haunts. After setting up the wall tent, cutting firewood and shooting a few arrows to get in rhythm, I headed out for the evening hunt.

Two days later I had yet to see, hear, bump or smell an elk. All I found were dozens of new two-tracks cut through prime hunting habit, tracks made by the ever increasing number of ATV users who abuse the wilderness in lieu of hard footwork. After an unsuccessful stalk on a mule deer buck, I decide it was time to head back to camp for an adult libation and to stare in the campfire.

The waning sun was casting darkening shadows from the tall subalpine fir and white pine trees as I pulled my way up through the deep hellhole I had found myself in. The aspen were changing, I noticed with some melancholy; winter was coming and I had not spent enough time in the woods. I felt deprived, as only one who loves to be outside can appreciate. The thought of cooking after dark wasn't appealing, so I tried to think of something quick so I could get into bed early; I wanted to be out before sunup the next day.

As I neared the top of the ridge a big blue grouse blasted from its hiding place in the huckleberries and lit in a well-branched fir. I came in close enough to put the glass on the tree and spotted the bird sitting broadside, giving me that side-glance like, "You can't see me!" Yeah, right!

I came to a point under the tree where I had a fairly open shot at the bird's breast and nocked an arrow. The bird had chosen to stay put so I calmly drew my bow and hit it dead center, breaking its back. It tumbled down through the branches, hit the ground and started to flop away, but it didn't make it far. It was a fine specimen, a beautiful bird, and my mouth watered as I planned for its culinary addition to dinner.

As I neared camp, two more blues lit into another tree. The first one spooked before I got to the tree, but the second bird sat still. I shot over its back, my arrow sailing off to parts unknown. But the second arrow took one bird low in the neck, cutting off its head, save for a thin strand of skin, sending it tumbling down to the ground.

The weight of the brace of blues on my belt felt good as I made my way back to camp in the alpenglow of a glorious fall evening. Oddly, I didn't feel so bad about not finding an elk.

Campfire Reflections ═══════════════════ **Seven**

Blindless Birds

Winters are hard on me. By the time the snow finally melts from the hills, and the cold air starts to warm a little, I get cabin fever so bad I need to escape. And nothing helps alleviate this desire more than getting out into the woods to chase turkeys.

I don't hold claim to being much of a turkey hunter, although I do spend a lot of time at it and have managed to bag a few birds. But I have learned a few things over the years and one of them is that turkey hunting can be quite a savage and frustrating endeavor, depending on your state of mind going into the thing. Finding a gobbler in the spring is relatively easy; getting it to come into your spread of decoys is much more difficult.

Ask a dozen seasoned turkey hunters the best way to kill a spring gobbler and you'll hear a dozen different techniques, although the basics will be the same: find the gobbler's roost, get in and set up before sunlight, spread your decoys out, and give hen yelps when the bird flies down from its roost. Simple, isn't it? For most turkey hunters I guess this works. However, I have never found hunting these birds a simple affair.

Over the years I have used ground blinds, treestands, camouflage netting and even a ghillie suit to hide myself when a gobbler comes into my decoys. Most of the time the bird sees my movement as I start to draw, and sometimes when I am lucky enough to get the bow back to full draw without being seen, I get so excited I flat out miss. But I like to still-hunt them every spring, and every so often I get lucky and bag one. So it was with great expectations, and a little curiosity, that I traveled to Colorado last spring to hunt with my friend Fred Eichler for turkeys.

"We'll kill birds," he said. "They're easy when you know how to hunt them!"

Yeah, right. I'd heard all this before. But still, my interest was piqued: Fred has a long list of birds under his belt and I wanted to learn a little more about his technique at bagging the wild turkey.

I arrived in Denver and Fred picked me up at the airport. It was hot for April; the temperature was in the upper 80s. Fred said the birds were talking and he had already called in over a half dozen birds that week. So I threw my duffel bag into the truck and we headed down toward Trinidad.

After setting up in a wall tent, we hiked up a hill behind camp to see if we could find a bird. Once we reached the end of an old logging road, Fred set up his Double Bull pop-up blind and placed a single hen decoy out about 15 yards in front. I had my reservations about this set-up. I couldn't believe a bird would walk up to this camouflage box and allow a sharp stick to be thrown at it from said box. Fred called and we waited...nothing happened. He called again and we waited...still nothing...not a sound. Dark came and we hiked back down to the tent. I was right, I thought. That blind scared the hell out of those birds! But the following morning I learned another thing about turkeys.

It was well before daylight when we set up the blind and decoy on the edge of a grassy knoll. Several toms were gobbling all around us, a good sign for sure. As pink light came Fred gave several yelps from a box call and set back. Immediately a tom boomed off to our right, then another behind the blind. I nocked an arrow and positioned myself to shoot out of one of the small windows in the blind. But after an hour the birds shut up and never showed themselves. I just knew it was the blind again.

"They'll be here," Fred assured me as his eyes slowly closed. Within a few minutes we were both asleep in our folding chairs.

A loud gobble roused me from my stupor and I looked out to see a tom on the other side of the knoll strutting around a hen. I yelped a few times and he stopped to look over at the decoy. Fred scratched a few yelps from the box call, but the tom wouldn't budge. However, the hen did—she came running up to the decoy, cackling and strutting around it, purring and looking like a cobra about ready to strike the damn decoy. She was so close I was about half tempted to reach out and grab her by the neck. But better sense told me I would probably get my butt kicked by the hen if I did, so I sat and watched the show. In the meantime the gobbler walked out of sight and never returned. Within a few minutes the hen got bored with the stuffy decoy and left as well.

Back in camp for lunch I heard a gobble down through the juniper and pinion trees and grabbed my bow. I figured I might as well try a stalk as nothing else was working. Not a hundred yards from camp I came across several gobblers strutting in an opening with about a half dozen hens. I crawled down a wash until I was less than 20 yards from them, but could not find a clear shot through the brush. As I waited for one of the toms to pass by the only opening I could get an arrow through, the sky clouded over and it began to snow, big time. The birds disappeared into the brush as bigger and bigger flakes came down.

The evening hunt was shot, and by the next morning it was evident the snow was not going to let up anytime soon, so we packed up camp and headed to Nebraska.

The snow had turned to rain by the time we hit the Nebraska border and after settling into a seedy hotel room we headed out to a ranch Fred had permission to hunt. The road was vulgar; mud was so thick it was hard to keep the truck from slipping off into the borrow pits. As we pulled into the ranch we could see several dozen birds in each of the coulees and after parking we hiked up into one of them and set up the blind and decoys.

It was a relief to be sitting in the blind out of the rain, but the noise of water pounding the canvas was deafening, making it hard to hear a gobbler if it was close, much less if it was anywhere beyond a couple dozen yards! We sat in the dark, damp air for what seemed to be several hours before the rain let up. Fred gave a few yelps and several gobblers boomed from the ridge to our right. I peeked out a slit in the blind and saw several birds making their way down the hill toward us. Something spooked them—I thought of the blind again—and they blew off back over the hill. One lone gobbler flew in the tree above us but never came down before darkness set in. It was a long ride back to our dingy hotel room. Hopefully the morrow would be clear and we would have better luck.

After we had both showered and dressed, I figured we'd run into town for some grub. "Everything's closed, Teej," Fred said. "That's OK, 'cuz I got some food here." He whipped out a one burner Coleman stove, lit the thing, and proceeded to cook our dinner right damn smack in the middle of our motel room floor! Of course, the meal of macaroni and cheese and canned fruit was not what I was planning on, but filling just the same.

Early the next morning we awoke to thunder and a torrential downpour. So much for a break in the weather. Another long ride through the hellish mud, a hike up into another coulee, and we set up once again. By the time we got into the blind we were soaked and cold, a thermos of coffee our only salvation from the elements.

Darkness finally gave way to a bruised sky as the storm continued to lash out. We heard nothing...saw nothing...and within a few hours I found myself falling in and out of sleep. This was just not fun, I thought as the rain continued to pour down so hard it started to find its way through the material of the blind.

Finally I had had enough and told Fred I was going to go out and find a bird to stalk. He agreed and we packed up and hiked up to the top of the ridge where we could look down each coulee. As if on cue, the sky started to open up and the rain stopped for the time being. But now the wind picked up and chilled me to the bone. Just as I was about to call it a day I looked over one last ridge and saw over a dozen turkeys sulking in the open grass down below. On the hill next to them were another ten or twelve birds. I glanced at Fred and said I was going to make a stalk. He smiled and said, "Go for it!"

It took a while to navigate through the trees, brush and mud and by the time I finally found the tree I had previously marked as my target the wind had reached a savage strength. Grass was lying over sideways as I crawled onto the crest of the hill, the noise of the wind deafening, the mud caked so hard into my clothing that I felt I was around 250 pounds. A few more feet and I could see the birds in the bottom of the coulee, but where were the others? I thought.

I had crawled over to where I figured the birds should have been, so I nocked an arrow and slowly rose on my knees as I peered down the hill. The grass was whipping back and forth toward me, the wind coming head on, when all of a sudden six or seven red, white and blue gobbler heads rose up in front of me. I looked to my right and there were several more birds looking at me. It was now or never.

I stood up quickly and picked out one bird as they all started running to the edge of the hill and taking wing. Just as the bird I had been following was spreading its wings, I sent a 4-blade Zwickey Delta-tipped arrow straight through its back. The bird blasted off the hill but instead of following the others it made a straight flight across the coulee. Just before it reached the safety of the trees on the other side, it folded up in mid air and crashed into a small creek in the bottom.

Fred came running up over the hill and asked what happened. I told him I had a bird down and he didn't believe me.

"You actually got a shot? And hit it?"

Please, Fred!

The tom only sported a three-inch beard, but it was a great coup for me; it was the second gobbler I had killed while stalking and the satisfaction of the experience was overwhelming. After a lot of jabbering and taking photos we headed back to the hotel. I was contemplating buying a second tag when the sky closed up and the rain began to fall again.

No, I was done and quite happy with my success. Taking the tom by stalking, after hunting in absolutely vicious weather for the week, was just too good and I wanted to savor the moment. Besides, I needed to get back home; our turkey season was just starting and I had to try out my new blind just to see if it would really work.

Eight
T.J. Conrads

On The Wing

Maryland

All I heard was, "Get ready!" the dog handler said as me and three other fellows prepared to shoot. With arrows nocked and ready, the handler nudged the pointer into the brush. Immediately a rooster cackled and rose several feet before leveling off and setting into afterburner mode. I drew, locked eyes on the roosters' mid section, and loosed broadhead-tipped flu-flu arrow. As if in slow motion, the arrow caught the bird square in the rear and exited just below its neck. The bird dropped from the sky as the other three arrows from my hunting buddies passed harmlessly through the air.

I was basking in my success, my three hunting buddies praising what a shot I was, when the dog went on point again. This time when the bird hit its apogee and began to take level flight, my arrow—along with the other three—missed the bird completely. That wasn't so bad, but the same thing happened on the next eleven shots! Needless to say, my heady place among the revered fell to the ground.

I don't claim to be any sort of aerial shooter, although I have hit the occasional flying disk and sand-filled milk jug. So when I nailed the first pheasant in flight that I ever shot at, I thought I must be doing something right. However, the next dozen shots met nothing but air, even though I did manage to shoot three birds out of the air by noon.

That first experience took place on a game preserve in Maryland. I was invited to speak to the Traditional Bowhunters of Maryland and one of the perks was several of the Board members had set me up for a pheasant hunt. Having never done such a thing, I wasn't sure what to expect. I had heard that it was challenging even though the birds are planted, and some folks had reservations about doing such a thing. What I found out was it wasn't that easy, and it takes a damn good dog to hold a bird long enough for a shooter to get in position. And above all, it was extremely exciting and challenging, and whet my appetite for more.

Africa

Bird life in Africa is astounding. I have personally identified over 300 species and have photographed several dozen. But of all the birds, doves are by far the most prolific. Sit at any source of water for more than a few minutes and you will have literally hundreds of birds come and water. Early in the morning and mid to late afternoon the doves come to water, and when they do you will be in for a treat.

On my first couple of trips to Africa I hunted doves and guinea fowl with a shotgun. One afternoon, Matthew, my PH, and I were sent out to secure a basket of doves for snacks in camp. Within two hours we had over 75 doves in the cooler, and a few very sore shoulders. As we were shooting the doves when they came in to water, I visualized how to shoot them with a bow. When I returned home that year, I bought a Snaro head, thinking that the large head would knock the stuffing out of a dove, the large piano wire loops giving me a wide surface area.

Through the following spring I shot the Snaro and found it lacking in flight characteristics. Even though I was using the smaller one—220 grains as compared to 280 grains—the arrow still flew head low, tail high. However, I was still hitting what I was aiming at, so armed with the Snaro and a handful of Judos, my trip to Africa found me wanting a close encounter with doves.

My first experience shooting doves with the Snaro-tipped arrow was a joke. I was trying to pass shoot them as they flew to water. The birds easily avoided the slow, heavy arrow, with flu-flu fletching, although I did manage to knock a few feathers off one or two. My strategy had to change.

My next attempt was to sit in a ground blind near water. A few singles came in, which I promptly missed in my excitement. I finally developed the theory that I had to shoot them just before they touched down. It would have been easy to kill several of them with one shot when they were all sitting there drinking, and I will have to admit that I did shoot a few that way—due to frustration—but I digress.

After several attempts and several near misses, I finally connected on an emerald spotted dove, one of the smaller species. It was like slow motion as the bird came in fast and then started to hover. At the hit all I saw were feathers—lots of them—where the bird used to be. I scrambled out of the blind and there, lying within a few yards, was my first dove! I snapped a few pictures and went back into the blind, but I didn't shoot another one that day, and it didn't matter; I had finally taken a dove on the wing!

By the end of the trip I had shot three, one of them with a Judo-tipped arrow as it lifted off from a spring. The rest of the folks in camp thought I was nuts....

Idaho

When I first moved to Idaho several decades ago, pheasant numbers were high and the hunting on private and public land was fabulous. I am not at all certain what changed—some say habitat loss by more effective farming, while another faction blames predators—but the sad reality is their numbers have declined considerably. Today, almost every Wildlife Management Unit in the state stocks farm raised birds for hunter consumption, and hunters have to pay for that privilege.

Years ago getting permission to hunt private land took a simple knock on a door and a smile. Today, you'd be hard pressed to find a friendly smile on the other side of that door unless you have a checkbook in hand. Farmers and ranchers who have any huntable game on their land know the value of that resource, and you can't blame them for trying to make a little money from it to make ends meet. Since most of us do not have the money to buy up land under a lease, or have access to private land, public land and wildlife management units are the norm.

Contrary to what many inexperienced bird hunters will tell you, hunting farm raised pheasants that have been released is far from shooting fish in a barrel. In some cases these birds are far more wily than their native-born brethren. But for the bowhunter, working these birds with a good dog can be as exciting as any bird hunting.

Molly and I were working a thick patch of cattails along the Snake River when her tail started to wag faster and she slowly moved forward. Being a retriever and not a pointer, I have come to appreciate the little nuances about her that tells me what she is up to. With an arrow nocked, I kept behind her about three paces when all of a sudden a cackle erupted from just ahead of her and a rooster rose above the reeds. The arrow was on its way...much too late, it seems...and the bird escaped unharmed. When the dog came back, she stared at me as if to ask why I didn't shoot. Being her first time behind a bow rather than a shotgun, it was a little hard for her to comprehend.

That was a special day. Although we did not kill a rooster, we had several shots and two long tail feathers for our efforts...success in my book! And even to date I have yet to kill an Idaho pheasant on the wing, but this season is looking quite promising.

I took Molly with me last year when I went after elk and deer. Many of my friends said I was crazy, but I know this dog better than I know most people, my family included. She is obedient, stays close, listens and pays attention, so I figured I would bring her along.

It wasn't her fault that I missed two bucks that trip; she stayed tight on my heels, watched the deer, and at the shot ran after the arrow, always finding it before I did. When in the final stalk on an animal, I'd have her stay and she would lie down, and wouldn't budge until I touched my leg, meaning she was to come to me.

One afternoon we worked down an old logging skid through some quaking aspens that usually held deer when several blue grouse lit into a fir. My first broadhead caught a large bird through the chest and it fell from the tree. Molly was quick to retrieve the bird, which still had my arrow sticking out of it, and I worried about her cutting herself. But she seemed to know better and walked slowly back with the bird proudly in her mouth. As is our ritual, I quickly gutted the bird and gave her the heart and liver as a reward.

By now the rest of the birds had skied to parts unknown, so we moved on down the ridge. Suddenly there was movement in front of me and several blue grouse where moving through the huckleberry bushes. I shot and hit one, which Molly went after, and the others ran down the hill. After retrieving the bird, Molly got her treat and we slowly worked down the ridge. Deer hunting was over; birds were the name of the game now.

Within ten minutes I spotted a large blue standing in the trail. As I prepared to shoot, it took wing straight away and I pulled up and shot without thinking. Imagine my surprise when the arrow zipped through the back of the grouse and out its neck! It continued to fly for about 20 yards, with Molly giving chase, then crumpled to the ground. I was in shock. Never before, in all the times I have shot at a grouse in the air, had I even taken a feather. Now I had one in my hand that was brought down by a cedar arrow and 4-blade Zwickey Delta.

Through trial and error I have come up with what I feel is the best arrow for shooting birds on the wing, and that is my normal 595 grain shaft with a 4-blade Zwickey Eskimo or Delta, with three fletch flu-flu feathers shot from my hunting bow. This combination gives me plenty of speed up to about 25 yards, which is much farther than I like to shoot, and the flu-flu fletching keeps the arrow from flying too far, for both safety and arrow retrievability concerns.

So far, I have taken three pheasants, several doves and one grouse on the wing with my longbow, and I have a strong urge to set up decoys this winter and try and shoot a few mallards from the air. No, it is not the most productive way to put meat on the table, but wing shooting with a bow has some sort of magic to it, and I can't wait to get back out there and try it again.

Big Game Adventures

Nine — T.J. Conrads

Post Season

It was cold...real cold. I had been sitting in a crouched position watching the big buck and his rather large collection of does for over 45 minutes. The low, bruised clouds above me had turned this draw of sage- and bitterbrush into a quiet, snow-covered arena. Every time I moved my body the deer would look up to where I was perched behind a clump of sage.

As I watched I could hear everything the deer were doing—the snap of bitterbrush being bitten off, each step placed on the powder of snow and the clash of antlers when one of the smaller bucks tried to get into the big boy's harem. I was relegated to remain in place and hope they would meander back up the draw past me. It was a nice buck I was watching, sporting four large, symmetrical tines on each side with good eye guards to boot. For the last five years I had been trying to outsmart a mulie of his proportions…and never won. Today looked like a page out of the past as I sat watching the buck, knowing I was pinned down, unable to move because of the stillness of this wintry arena.

Just when I thought I could no longer stay put in my uncomfortable position, the does started to move right up the draw toward me. Ever so slowly I nocked an arrow and shifted my weight slightly downhill toward where I figured they would pass by. My hope was that the wind would hold, the does would pass, and the big buck would follow, allowing me one opportunity to let the air out of him.

The first doe came strutting through two large clumps of sagebrush not 20 yards away. Looking down the draw I saw the buck round up the rest of his does and head up toward the lead doe.

"Settle down, buddy. Take a breath…relax!" I mumbled to myself as the situation started to come together. Right! I've never been able to control my nerves around large mulies before…why start now?

Another doe filtered through the opening in the brush and I felt the string tighten against my fingers. Single file they came, and each time one of them walked by, I pulled a little harder at the Flemish string. Finally the buck appeared and, as if by magic, he stopped and looked down the hill. With not much thought, the bow came up, my anchor point hit, and the arrow was on its way.

At the sound of the string being released, the buck dropped to gather his feet and the arrow zipped just over his back. The game was over and I had lost…again.

I love hunting mule deer, not just because they are the prevalent deer species where I live, but because they inhabit the best of what the West has to offer—open sage flats, large expanses of untouched wilderness, and some of the most majestic and aesthetically pleasing country to be found anywhere. And the vast majority of their home range is on public land where a gate or property owner does not control access.

It has been said that mule deer are stupid as compared to a whitetail, but I beg to differ. Obviously, small mule deer bucks are easy to kill, but once they get past a certain age and size, like a decent four point or better, you have met your match. First of all, unlike a whitetail that lives in a small area and will hide and change its route, jump a big-antlered mule deer once and he's gone. Period. Which is the main reason why mule deer have been declining in the West: they do not like to coexist with whitetail deer or humans. Destroy their habitat by construction, or introduce a more adaptable species such as the whitetail, mule deer will either die off or move. They like to live a loner's life.

Hunting mule deer in the late season, or the post season as it is called in some places, is an exhilarating experience. The mountains have taken on the covering of winter's white blanket and the mule deer are experiencing their annual need to procreate. The result is deer moving down to their winter range, with bucks chasing does in what can only be called be a comical display of male chauvinism. It seems that everywhere you look you can see deer. Not just your average sized deer, but tremendous mulie bucks...in deep rut.

Most of the western states that allow late archery seasons do so for good reason. Mule deer spend most of the year in high, rugged country where they do not encounter a lot of hunting pressure. Because of this the herds generally become over populated. When winter rolls around they head down to lower elevations to find food, which usually happens to be some rancher's hay barn or field, as well as areas that are full of bitterbrush, a main winter staple. These late seasons permit bowhunters to harvest out part of the herds and to keep the deer away from ranches—thus the name "depredation hunts."

Post seasons usually follow the rifle season by about two to three weeks, giving the deer plenty of time to relax from being chased all over the country by wild-eyed folks in blaze orange. They now have their minds set on reproducing and will come down out of the high country to find a release for the build-up of hormones in their bodies. If you happen to be in the right area, you will literally see hundreds of deer every day.

Some of the best hunts I've taken have been in migration areas—ridges and foothills that lead to the mule deer's wintering grounds. Sitting on a ridge and glassing into draws, I've watched numerous bucks work their way down to the lower ground. Because of the terrain—mostly sagebrush and sparse pine and fir—you can spot the deer you want and then work your way into an ambush set-up.

This time of year is cold, so you will need to prepare yourself for the onslaught of snow, wind and freezing temperatures. My normal late season gear includes wool pants over Thermax long underwear, wool stocking cap, wool shirt and a wool jacket. Boots are a matter of preference...mine being a good set of insulated Danner's or the excellent Schnee's boot. Just remember that you may be standing in a foot of snow for extended periods of time and your feet *will* get cold after a while.

Mule deer inhabit big, open country where the use of optics is essential. Having both a pair of binoculars and spotting scope will allow you to set and glass lots of country looking for deer. I personally don't care to pack a spotting scope around all day in my hunting pack, so I have invested in a good pair of 10 X 40 roof prism binoculars. They allow me to glass large expanses of country and are easy on my neck after a day of walking the hills. Just remember, you get what you pay for when buying optics, so buy the best you can afford. You won't be sorry.

If you are lucky, as I am, you may only live an hour or two from excellent mule deer hunting areas. But in the event you will drive a long way to hunt these western nomads, proper shelter is a must. A canvas wall tent with a wood stove provides an excellent base camp to hunt out of. You can place one just about anywhere you find flat ground. Most of the country you hunt mulies in is somewhere near the fringe area-between the timbered foothills and the lower sagebrush. Finding wood for fires and shelter from the wind is not a problem.

The key to finding big bucks in the post season is knowing where to look for them. One year I took my father out hunting in an area that I had been passing by for years. It was close to my house and I never thought of looking for any deer there. Dad sat glassing from his perch on a high ridge while I walked up the ridge to look over into another bowl. As I worked through the bowl I found many sets of dropped antlers...big antlers! The more I combed the area, the more I found, along with lots of dried droppings.

Although I didn't see any deer on that excursion, I knew that this had to be either a migration route or a wintering ground. It was just below the fringe area of an unroaded expanse of National Forest land. Below, about ten miles, were ranches and farmland. The gears were turning.

I returned five weeks later when the late bow season was underway. I left the truck and made my way back to the bowl under some of the thickest fog I've ever seen. I knew that once I got there I wouldn't be able to spot any deer even if they were 20 yards away.

Reaching the top of the ridge I sat down and pondered the situation. As I sat there the fog rolled up into the forest and exposed the countryside. First one and then another deer popped into view. Within ten minutes I had spotted three bucks...needless to say, my encounter with the biggest one was less than what I had hoped for. And although I didn't collect a deer that day, I did learn where to look for big bucks.

The following weekend I returned, determined to get another chance at the big buck. Crawling into the bowl I again found several other deer, but not the big boy. I hunted all day without seeing him again, but I was seeing many more deer than the week before.

The next morning I crawled out of my sleeping bag to meet a fresh layer of snow on the ground. After a cup of coffee, I headed back up the ridge to glass into the bowl. As I worked my way back up the hill I noticed several well-beaten trails heading down the mountain, past my truck and out into the lower foothills. I glassed from my usual spot at the head of the draw and saw several different deer than what I saw the day before.

It finally dawned on me; I was not hunting in a wintering area, but a local overnight rest stop for these winter travelers. They were heading down into the lower foothills, across the river, and into the sage flats of the Snake River plain to spend the winter...and I was going down after them.

The following weekend I took off to hunt a series of ridges above the sage flats. It was good winter range—lots of sagebrush and bitterbrush. I had just come around a finger ridge, which led into the sage covered basin, when a group of does bolted off the top of the ridge. I looked up to see what had pushed them when a decent buck appeared over the top. He looked down into the flats and then back at the does before strutting down across the ridge in front of me.

When he was about 25 yards away he stopped and looked over at the does again. That was my cue. In one fluid motion I swung the bow up and loosed the cedar shaft. The flight was good, but the arrow was too low. He jumped up the hill and stopped to look back where I was. I stood motionless in the sagebrush until he disappeared over the ridge.

Taking up the trail, I found him over the other side looking down into a deep gorge. I slipped within five yards of where he stood behind a rock and sent an arrow through both lungs and out the other side. His pell-mell run down the steep draw ended within 75 yards.

I had won...this time. He had made the mistake of letting his guard down and I was able to take advantage of it. I sat there in the snow for several long minutes admiring the antlers and the animal. Five years of hard hunting led up to this very moment, and I didn't want the adventure to end just yet. But I was more than a mile from my truck, in snow over a foot deep, and I needed to take care of the task at hand. Several hours later, after dragging the buck up and out of the draw, then across the sage flats, I dropped down to the road where I could bring the truck around. The sun was just settling across the Owyhee Mountains to the southwest as I slammed the door and turned the key, heading toward home. It had been a good season.

It has been several years since that hunt took place, and much has changed in that time. As is relative to most of the world, human population is expanding, and with that comes an increased number of hunters. Unfortunately, that means finding quality areas to hunt mule deer is becoming harder each year. However, I still look forward to the post season, and for snow to fall, when I spend much of my time searching out small, hidden creases in the foothills where a few smart mule deer always seem to be, trying to escape the influx of hunters. And each year I find another small area where the deer hide, where the new-age bowhunter refuses to walk to, and I have it all to myself once again.

When the snows blow this December, and the temperature hovers around the zero mark, I'll be putting on my wools and heading back to the lowland sage flats. For once again I'll be playing the game with these post-season mulies.

Ten == *T.J. Conrads*

Across The River

The rain was pelting me unmercifully as I sat in my treestand overlooking a series of scrapes I had located several days earlier. I had a hard time rationalizing just exactly why I was here, smack dab in the middle of some of the finest elk country in Idaho, during deer rifle season, waiting for a whitetail buck to come by. Being a mule deer hunter, and never having pursued whitetails before, this was all foreign to me. However, I had read all I could about whitetail deer and spent the time scouting this area all summer and early fall, so I felt fairly confident something would happen...but when was another story.

As the rain slowly seeped through my woolens, I decided to try and rattle, so after a few cracks of my rattling antlers and a few tinklings of the of tines, I sat back to see what would transpire. To my surprise, a cow elk cruised right by me. Then two more fed through the brush behind my aerie in a white pine. But no deer.

The rain continued to come down and once again I worried the antlers together, following up with a few grunts from a friction caller. No sooner had I finished the grunts than a doe came flying by my stand with a small fork-horn buck fast on her tail...literally. To a mule deer hunter on his first hunt for whitetail, this was something out of the ordinary, and extremely exciting, but after another hour of rain and more rattling and grunting it was time to head back to camp and get warmed up. Tomorrow would be another day.

I prefer to hunt mule deer. Roaming the high desert and sub-alpine regions of southern Idaho, longbow in hand, stalking big-racked mulies is what I enjoy most. And even though Idaho has a large population of whitetail deer, their northern locations and long distance from my home in Boise usually mean that I forgo excursions into whitetail areas and spend my time chasing my beloved mule deer. This year was different. I had made the decision to spend my time learning all I could about whitetails and put forth all my effort to try and bag one. I read all I could about their habits, talked to well-known whitetail gurus, and spent all summer and early fall scouting whitetail habitat trying to find an area where I would have the best opportunity to waylay one. The main rut for whitetail deer in Idaho occurs around the middle of November, and that meant I would have to hunt during the general season when all the rifle hunters are in the woods. Finding a quiet—and safe—place to hunt would be paramount.

During a scouting trip in late September I came across a 5-point buck that had been shot—and lost—a few weeks earlier during the early bow season. The expandable broadhead on an aluminum shaft was missing all its blades; the deer had died from a puncture wound in its stomach. It seemed like such a waste; the skeleton was lying under a small cedar, the aluminum arrow laced through the hindquarter and into its paunch. The deer had sought refuge under this cedar where it took its last breath only to rot away.

I pulled out the bone saw from my fannypack and removed the

antlers. They seemed just right for a set of rattling horns. Once I returned home I cleaned them up, drilled holes through each base, and tied them together with a leather cord. These, I thought, would be perfect for rattling in a horny buck. Time would tell.

One day a few weeks before the gun season opened, I decided to take a break from all the hiking and scouting and drove down to the river to cast a few flies to the steelhead that were wending their way upriver to spawn. Knee-deep in the clear, cool water, I watched several fish passing by in the shadows. I couldn't find a fly they wanted, but I didn't care; this was much-needed medicinal time more than anything, and the cool breeze moving up the river and the golden hues of aspen along the bank were more than satisfying as I roll-cast my line toward an undercut on the far bank.

I was daydreaming when something caught my eye. There, on the other side of the river, was a fairly decent whitetail buck making its way across the steep side of the hill not 50 yards away. I watched as he slowly moved into the thick timber that snaked up into the crags above me, a place I had yet to see anyone else in, much less even crossed my mind to scout. Since the fish were not cooperating, I packed the fly rod and waded the river to find out what lay beyond.

Once across the river I climbed up a steep bank that led me to a treed flat with a creek meandering through it. Several trails crisscrossed the flat, running up steep hills into the forest on both sides. I decided to investigate further. Up one trail I came to a knob that overlooked the river. On this knob were a series of seven fresh scrapes, as well as one scrape that was almost four feet in diameter. Several small pine trees had fresh rubs and a half dozen trails fanned out through the ferns and trees. This, I mused, is where I had to be. I cleared out an area for a ground blind and cut limbs from a pine for a treestand. Now I had to wait another two weeks for the general season to open.

The day before the gun season opened I drove north and pitched my tent in the last spot in a campground on the river in a horrible rainstorm. Several other rigs and trailers were parked at the far end of the campground, which I gathered were gun hunters. The weather had been awful for the last week and the river was several feet higher than when

I had forded it several weeks earlier. But I had expected such and had packed a raft and oars. Under the cover of darkness that evening, I quietly pumped up the raft and hid it among the willows along the river below my camp. I didn't want anyone to know that I was hunting across the river, so stealth and cunning were very important.

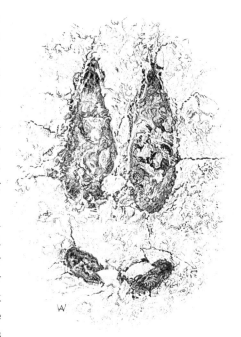

I awoke to rain beating on the sides of the tent; the wind had picked up considerably overnight. Gathering all my gear, I made my way in the dark down to the river and loaded the raft. The crossing was hazardous enough with the high water, but the wind added another interesting element to the endeavor; I was drawn down stream several dozen yards farther from my expected landing spot and almost through a set of nasty rapids.

After pulling the raft back upstream and stashing it amongst the brush, I loaded my hunting pack and treestand and started slogging up the hillside in the dark. By the time I made the little flat I was caked with mud, soaking wet, and having second thoughts about what I was doing, so I took refuge under a large fir and waited for light.

The blackness soon gave way to gray light and eventually I could see enough to climb up out of the flat to the knob I had previously found. The pine I had picked out would allow me to cover a major trail that crossed the knob as well as the hillside above and set my treestand in amongst its limbs. Farther down the trail I built a brush blind that would work if the predominate wind switched. It was mid-morning by the time I finished so I climbed up into my stand for a few hours just to get a feel for the place.

From my perch in the pine tree I could see down both sides of the knob as well as over much of the brush that hid several scrapes. Above me was a fairly open fern-covered hill, and behind, almost a hundred yards below me, the river bubbled over several large boulders. It felt like a perfect set-up, except for the rain pouring down. I rattled and grunted off and on for the entire day without seeing a thing, so I climbed down and headed back to the raft at dark, and rowed back to camp for dinner and my sleeping bag.

For the next two days the rain fell and the river rose several more inches. I saw several elk and a few deer, but I wasn't getting any shot opportunities. Every deer I saw was either chasing a doe, or being chased by a buck. To compound my frustration, each crossing was more treacherous; I had to launch from farther up the river to make sure I didn't drift down through the rapids. One morning I was almost busted by one of the gun hunters as he came out of his trailer to relieve himself over the bank as I hid below in the reeds by the river.

Good grief! I thought. This was just becoming too much.

I awoke on the fourth day to quiet...no rain or wind. I crawled out of my sodden tent to greet a soupy fog that breathed down the river. I quickly dressed, drank a cup of instant coffee, and made another push across the river into the great unknown. It is amazing just how fast you can row when you can't see the other side!

Up in the tree well before the darkness gave way to gray light, I heard several hoofed animals running through the quiet darkness. Then antlers crashed farther up the hill. I sat back, zipped up my wool coat, and waited for enough light to see.

The rain started up again but only lasted for an hour or so. As soon as it stopped, the forest came alive. A red fox trotted by through the dark ferns, and a cow and calf elk fed right by me. Gray jays swooped through the trees and one lit on a branch above me, giving me the "big eye" as it cocked its head back and forth. It was a pleasant time and soon the sun came out for the first time all week. It was time to dry out.

Grabbing the rattling horns, I gave a few cracks and followed up with a few tine rubs and then a low grunt. I had no sooner hung the antlers up when a small 5x5 buck ran down the hill and stood looking past my tree. He stared for several minutes and then turned broadside. I slowly pulled an arrow from my quiver and turned toward him. As he started to walk away, I slipped an arrow through his rib cage and he tore

Campfire Reflections 63

off into the thick woods. It happened so fast I never had time to think about it. By the time I hung my bow onto a broken limb, my legs were starting to quiver.

I found the buck dead behind a wide spruce tree where he died on the run. He wasn't huge, but he was the first whitetail I had ever killed and I was ecstatic. One of his tines was shaped like an acorn, giving him a queer, unique look. After several minutes of admiring the deer, I quickly gutted him, tossed the heart and liver into a Zip-Lock bag, and drug him down to the river where I shot a few pictures, loaded him into the raft, and made my way back across the river to camp. It was time to go home with my hard-earned trophy.

Eleven — *T.J. Conrads*

The Bowl

Every Bowhunter Has That Special Place...

I've always liked this place. The deep pockets of Douglas fir, spruce and pine have an abundance of small seeps in their understory that seem to attract elk and deer during the hot days of summer and fall. Even during the drought years there is always water oozing out of the ground, nourishing the wild currents, huckleberries and grasses that the animals feed on. Spruce, ruffed and blue grouse frequent the bowl, and add a welcomed bounty to my annual sojourn here.

I have spent many seasons here hunting for elk, but mostly just letting my mind settle down from the rat race of earning a living in town. The pace is slow...refreshing...allowing me the chance to recharge my soul and gain back the feeling that comes over a person when he is at peace with their world. A world where everything happens much too fast.

I discovered this place one year while passing through the area looking for some small lake I had found on a topographic map. I had stopped to stretch my sore muscles—something that comes from spending too many hours behind the wheel of a four-wheel-drive—when I spotted a slight depression in the side of the mountain. It looked like a place that an elk would love. So, I grabbed my grunt tube and headed over to the rim that surrounded the depression.

The view was fantastic. From the top of the cliff I could see the entire bowl as it cascaded down towards the farmland below. Small, open meadows were splashed across the bowl, adding a sense of openness, yet seclusion. It was late in the afternoon, and I didn't really expect to hear a reply to my bugle. Breathing in a full breath of air, I gave the reed all I had, finishing with the standard grunts afterwards. Immediately an elk sounded off deep from within the tangle of timber. Then another call came back to me, but this one was farther up the opposite side of the bowl. Back to the truck I went, gathering up my fannypack, bow and slamming down a sandwich before diving off the top of the rim. Destiny was calling me.

Although I never got into those two bulls that evening, I have returned to this spot every year since then, always encountering elk and mule deer. It still amazes me that I've never had any company...the un-welcomed kind, anyway. A ridge road runs all the way around the western side of the bowl, and many times as I have been immersed in its black timber I have heard other bowhunters bugle down into it. But the terrain and thickness of the timber keeps most of them from even entering the uppermost fringes.

Over the years I've been able to hunt this area by myself, making camp back in the spruce and fir trees well off the ridge road. It's a pleasant feeling sitting in camp enjoying a break from hunting and see rigs drive past every now and then. The hunters never stop to see what lies beyond the road. So my little private piece of the mountain has remained a bowhunter's paradise for one of my closest friends and me. Some years I venture into new areas, but I always seem to end up back here. Many memories of past hunts—successes and failures—pull me into the bowl each season. I'm sure there are better areas to hunt on this mountain, but I like this spot. And I always get into game.

This year was to be different. I had decided to take my eight-year-old son, Travis, with me hunting the opening weekend. The main concern I had was to allow him the opportunity to see some elk in the wild. Since I have always been able to find elk in this area, the task seemed feasible...maybe I'd even get an opportunity for a shot.

Besides, having him along would keep me from blasting through the woods, something that usually takes me a couple of days to get over once I get out of town. I just needed to get away for a few days. And a few days were all we had; school started on Monday.

My good friend and hunting companion, Nick Nydegger, and his wife and son were to meet up with us on Saturday afternoon. Nick has been my hunting partner for many years, and we've shared many great hunts in the bowl. This year his son, Ben, was going on his first hunt at the ripe old age of 12.

Friday evening found Travis and me setting up camp, getting ready for the opening morning. This would give us a chance to settle in and for me to show Travis around the area. I had to make sure that he enjoyed himself; the first hunting experiences for kids must be enjoyable, or they may never learn to like the sport. Travis has been shooting a bow since the age of four, and he opted to take his custom longbow along. We had a blast, shooting at pinecones and thistles.

After dinner we went for a walk around a small bluff just outside camp, talking about our plans for the following morning. As we came to a small cluster of pines, a beautiful 4X4 mule deer buck stood up about 20 yards away from us. He got an eyeful of these two characters and blew off the bluff into the timber on the other side of the ridge road. Within five minutes, a coyote came trouncing over the hill and came to a sudden stop in the sagebrush. Travis was enjoying this scene immensely, talking wildly and pointing fingers at the coyote. The coyote, too, soon had enough of our human presence and ran off in the same direction he had come. It was a pleasurable evening, and we both talked about it for many hours around the campfire that night. I was already feeling relaxed and was looking forward to getting into the bowl in the morning.

Before turning in, I showed Travis how I sharpen my broadheads. I was trying a new one this year—Wolverines, which had been sent to me by Harry Elburg. They took an edge nicely, surprising Travis at how they could shave hair off my forearm.

Soon after sunup, I grabbed my new Robertson longbow and shot a few arrows to limber up my muscles. The old arrow stump was still just as hard as last year; it claimed one of my Judo tips. A quick breakfast and Travis and I headed off down the trail leading into the bowl.

As we crested the first rise, I saw an un-welcomed sight; there was a bowhunter standing at the edge of the bowl, looking back across a large meadow, with an arrow nocked on his bow. When we came up to this guy, he was mumbling something about putting an arrow in an elk and his friend was up the hill trying to flush it down to him. I asked if he had been into the draw, and he said he hadn't. Glad that he hadn't ruined the area for us, we hurried down the trail. I knew that we had to get over to the other side of the bowl before these two characters scared the elk out. There are two main escape routes out of the bowl which elk use, and we were headed there as fast as we could.

It was quiet in the timber, except for the gurgling of many small seeps and streams. As we padded down a well-used trail, I explained to Travis about trying to walk quietly. It was hard for him, but he managed to stay fairly quiet. We plodded along, crossing the largest stream before heading up the other side.

About 50 yards from the lower escape trail, the sound of pounding hooves and branches breaking echoed through the trees. Six to eight elk ran across in front of us, obviously spooked by the other hunters. Quickly placing a reed in my mouth, I gave a loud cow call. The elk kept on running, never being close enough to hear me. As they crested the top, a spike came by, much closer to us. I squealed as he ran by us and he stopped and squealed back. Down he came, almost 15 yards in front of us before he spotted something strange. I called again and he turned around, looking up the hill where the other elk had run, then looked back at us. All of a sudden another elk ran up and I squealed again. This was a large cow, almost half again as large as the spike.

Already having an arrow nocked, I aimed for her mid section and loosed the shaft. It disappeared through her a little too high, I thought. She banged up against a small pine tree and dashed right by us, disappearing down through the trees. As I listened, I heard the brush breaking and then all was silent. Looking back at the tree, I saw bright red blood splashed down the trunk.

"You shot her, Dad! Did you see the arrow?" Travis had watched the whole episode unfold before him, and never said a word until then.

"Uh huh," I mumbled, not believing all this could happen within an hour from camp on opening morning. I've had shots on opening day before, but something always seemed to go wrong. This was turning out much different.

All this time the spike was still standing there, not ten feet from where the cow was when I shot. I'm not sure what was going through his mind, but he obviously wasn't worried about it. With the reed still in my mouth, I called to him again and he came right up in front of us. There was no cover between him and us, just grass with the wind blowing down the hill from behind him. I could have slapped him in the head with my longbow.

"Dad!...Dad! He's getting closer!" Travis screamed as he grabbed onto my leg. This spike had absolutely no fear of us. I couldn't believe it. We continued our dialogue for about two to three minutes before the spike had enough and walked back up the hill, chirping the whole way. What a great experience this was, not only for me, but also for my son. I had succeeded in showing him some elk, and had shot one to boot.

Sitting down, I explained to Travis that we had to wait for 30 minutes before starting to track the cow. This he had a hard time understanding. He saw the arrow go through, and he saw the blood on the tree.

"Why can't we just go get it?"

He was learning.

The blood trail was easy to follow, as I had clipped the right lung and severed the femoral artery just under the spine. Too high, but still a good shot. I showed Travis how to blood trail and we soon walked up to the cow. She had gone about 75 yards at full bore, piling up on a small bench. I looked at my watch; it was almost 9:00 a.m., opening day and I had an elk on the ground. Maybe bringing Travis along had brought me good luck.

After field dressing and propping the elk open in the cool breeze by the stream, we headed back to camp to get the pack frame. Shortly after we arrived in camp, Nick drove up and he got the whole story from Travis. What timing! It's great to have help packing out an animal as big as an elk.

By mid afternoon, we had the elk quartered, bagged and hanging in the trees back in camp. Nick and his son, Ben, headed down into the bowl while I cleaned up and took a nap. It had been a hard, but productive, morning and I wanted to relive the day's events.

That afternoon Travis and I made a short hunt back over to where we had seen the buck the night before. We sat on the edge of a steep ridge, watching a Coopers hawk hunting overhead until darkness pushed us back to camp and a well-deserved dinner of elk tenderloin.

The next morning Travis and I headed back into the bowl to look for deer, hoping to see some mulie bucks. The day was warm and there was a cool breeze lifting up from deep within the dark timber. There is an old cow trail that snakes down from the ridge, through the drainage to the farmland below. Years ago the ranchers used this trail to move their cattle from the high meadows to the rich farmland below before the snows blew. Winters are long and hard here, and drifts can measure up to 16 feet in the basins. We encountered a few deer every now and then, but not any good bucks. It was a leisurely walk, and we were enjoying the sights.

There's a bench where I have jumped many an elk, and we snuck up to the edge and looked over into it. As I scanned the area, a cow elk stood up and began meandering down the side of the flat bedding area. Then there were two more, a spike and another cow. Travis took the whole scene in, never saying a word...maybe logging it for future use, I hoped.

Down the trail we came across a familiar sight to me. I remembered this spot from many years back. Dropping down off the trail, I came to a small pine tree. The marks were much bigger than I remembered, but they were very much identifiable. That day back then, I was walking back to camp after a day's hunting and turned my head to look down off the trail. Two spike elk were bedded right behind this tree. It was much smaller then, though. I can still see the spike I shot at as if it were just yesterday. He was lying broadside, glancing up at me and back at his buddy next to him. The sun was at my back, so I'm sure they didn't recognize what I was. The orange blur of the feathers buried right where I aimed. I never saw the small, inch and half sapling. But there it was, the scar left from digging out the Delta broadhead that had completely penetrated the sapling. The pine was now over four inches in diameter. And it holds yet another memory of this place for me.

We had just about come to another trail that led back to camp when all hell broke loose. Three or four blue grouse flushed from under a small bush in front of us. The poor boy just about came unglued. He jumped back and yelled something...maybe swearing, I think. I laughed and watched as the grouse flew into the surrounding pines. One of them had perched on a low limb in one of the trees, providing a good backstop for a Judo—the trunk. Blues are normally a very nervous bird, always putting plenty of country between them and me. This guy wasn't too smart. I knew I could hit him. Out came a Judo-tipped shaft and off went the arrow. It was a good shot, the shaft flying true, straight through the bird and implanting itself in the tree. Perfect! I don't climb trees anymore than I have to, but this one had my number on it. By the time I got the damn thing down I looked as if I'd been in a catfight. Travis enjoyed the show, with Dad trying his hardest to look like the skilled outdoorsman he said he was. And I am. It's just that I'm not as young as I used to be and climbing bare trees is not my forte these days.

Nothing hurt but my pride, I proceeded on showing my laughing son the plumage on the blue. I pulled out the longest tail feather and stuck it in my hat.

"Why'd you do that?" Travis asked.

"It's sort of good luck, I guess. Kind of weird, but it's just that I have been doing it for so long now, it's kind of a ritual." How do you explain the strange customs that evolved from hunting experiences to a young boy? Maybe I'm one of the few, but I know there are others who have this strong urge to embed memories of the hunt in themselves. Kind of like putting the good luck arrow in the tree at camp each year, hoping to appease the gods of the hunt, or hunting the same spots where past animals have fallen to one of my arrows. There is a tall fir down in the belly of this bowl that has one of my arrows stuck high in its trunk. If someone ever sees it they are going to think somebody must have been an awful shot to place it so far up there. But I know how it got there and why. The first elk I ever killed fell at the base of that tree.

I noticed Travis putting a feather in his hat.

It was about noon when we strode back into camp, grouse carried high by a young man exposed to the wonderful world of hunting. Lunchtime, I thought. Mmmm..."Trav', would you get me a beer...and get yourself a soda, too." We ate a sandwich and talked about the morning's hunt.

After a short nap, I brought out my Strunk yew selfbow and braced it. Travis got out his longbow I had Ron Robison make for him for his fifth birthday a few years back and we shot arrows around camp. It felt good being in camp during the day for a change. This was turning out to be a relaxing trip, something I definitely needed.

I launched an arrow at a pinecone dangling from a low branch and watched as it careened off and sailed into a small stand of fir on the far side of camp. Fetching the arrow, I jumped a doe from her bed. She had been there, not 50 yards from camp, the whole time. She bounded up the side of the hill, looked back at us and casually walked into another stand of fir. Looking at the yew bow, and realizing I had never taken an animal with it, I thought about pursuing the deer. But I had already taken an elk and was planning on saving my tag for a big buck. The urge to shoot a deer with the selfbow overcame any feelings I had of antlers. It was just too much.

I walked back over to camp and grabbed my back quiver, telling Travis to grab the fannypack; we were going to stalk a deer! I snuck up to the stand of trees the doe had just entered and peered into the dark shadows, with Travis slightly behind me. It seemed like forever before I saw the doe. She was standing on the other side, silhouetted against the valley below. I nocked an arrow, looking for a clear lane when she stepped forward, giving me a broadside shot. I don't remember much...an orange flash as the arrow passed completely through her and she was gone.

"You got her, Dad!" I forgot he was standing right there. Scared the hell out of me when he yelled.

"Yeah," I replied, trying to remember the orange ball dashing through the darkness and out the other side. "Let's go back to camp and

The orange-feathered shaft passed completely through the doe.

get the pack frame, and we'll come back and trail her."

Having showed my son how to blood trail the elk the day before, I thought I would give him the opportunity to apply what he had learned. I knew the shot was a good one; the arrow had penetrated tight behind the shoulder and completely exited the other side. We walked around to where the doe had been standing when the arrow had hit her. Not finding any blood, I told Travis to look for hair, explaining that the broadhead would shave hair off the deer as it entered. He immediately found tufts of hair on the grass, and then the first blood a few feet from there.

Trying to savor the experience, I let him do all the tracking, keeping an eye on the spore myself. We had gone about 15 yards when he picked up the feathered end of the shaft. It was covered with bright red, frothy blood—a good hit for sure. He lost the trail when the deer had run across a hard-packed section of dirt littered with boulders.

"Look for her hoof marks in the dirt," I said, explaining that a running deer would churn up the earth. Soon he was back on track and found the broadhead end of the shaft. We were walking down a short embankment, my son's eyes glued to the crimson trail, when he almost fell over the doe. She had expired 60 yards from where I had shot her. Travis was overjoyed in the feeling of accomplishment, and I swelled with pride, too. He had just tracked his first arrow-hit animal, with success.

She wasn't a large deer, but one that I was proud to take. To experience success again, with my son by my side, using a yew selfbow, was another memorable experience, and a step back in time for me. A time when all fathers shared the hunt with their sons. And I was the proudest father on the mountain today.

Pictures were in order and after a short session we dressed the deer, loaded it onto the pack frame and headed for camp. Nick was there to greet us, giving me a hard time for thinning the animals out of the bowl so fast. It was all in jest, though, as he was beaming with happiness at our success. Nick and I have shared this spot for so many years, and now we were handing it down to our sons. What better way is there to keep our hunting tradition alive?

That evening we ate grouse and deer tenderloin, drank to success and sang songs around the campfire while Nick played his ever-present guitar—another ritual we have. The stars were bright as usual, and I hated to think about heading back home in the morning. I had come up here with the intention of finding some elk for Travis to see, hoping to get a chance to harvest one with my son by my side. I couldn't have choreographed it any better. I wanted this feeling to last forever. And it will in my memories.

The bowl had provided another memorable—but short—hunt. I had taken two animals in two days with two different bows, something that will probably never happen again. But I shared this with my son, and that will forever be one of the highlights of my life. I only hope that someday Travis will be able to share the same experiences with his son here. And I hope I'm still around to hunt this wonderful place.

Twelve
T.J. Conrads
True North Adventure

The drone of the twin engine Otter was trying to put me to sleep, but the thrill of the adventure was too overpowering. Below, all I could see was a multitude of lakes, and very little land. As I squinted my eyes through the aged and weathered Plexiglas window, I was imagining herds of caribou walking around down there. The more I studied the terrain, the more I saw—lots of rocks that were changing from cold, solid glacial debris to walking, living caribou.

My eyes must be working overtime, I thought, as I leaned back into the seat to relax. The chatter of excited bowhunters engulfed the cabin with laughter and stories of past hunts.

"Well, you gonna shoot one of these critters?" Glenn said as I turned to survey our group.

"Yeah," I replied, slowly bringing a smile to face. "Yeah, I think so."

As the pilot feathered the prop, we started our descent towards a group of brown and yellow cabins built on a sand spit next to Mackay

Lake. This was to be our home for the next seven days, hunting the Central Canada Barren Ground caribou and fishing for massive Lake trout. As we neared the runway, the grey rocks actually started to change, and some of them sported the racks we came to see.

Gary Jaeb owns and operates True North Safaris out of Yellowknife in the Northwest Territories of Canada. His hunting camp boasts an over 90% success rate on mature caribou bulls, not to mention the fabulous Lake trout and grayling fishing. Along with his wife, Bertha, and the many guides and camp personnel, Gary's Mackay Lake Lodge can accommodate up to 20 hunters a week. With so much territory, a bowhunter can hunt literally for days without running into another hunter. And the accommodations are superb.

This was a special hunt, as my two business partners, Larry Fischer and Wade Carstens, and I had booked this hunt with Glenn St. Charles and his two sons. At 81, Glenn was to be our senior member of a most impressive group of 15 bowhunters.

After we had secured our gear in the cabins, lunch was served and then the spotting scopes came out. Jack Joseph had locked onto a small band of large bulls feeding around the other side of the boat launch and was smiling from ear to ear with high expectations. The rest of the afternoon was spent whittling out the vitals of the caribou target. Russ Tye, Nathan Andersohn and Dale Holpainen went out for an afternoon fishing excursion, bringing back a cooler full of large Lake trout. The orange colored flesh made for a delightful meal. After dinner, we had a chance to meet and get to know our guides for the next six days of hunting. Joe St. Charles and I were assigned Bobby, a Dene Indian, as our guide.

The wind had whipped the lake to a frothy soup by early morning. As I stared out onto the lake I couldn't help but feel a little apprehensive about crossing it in a 16-foot aluminum boat, but that's what Bobby had in mind; we were going over to the other side.

We sighted numerous caribou right out of camp. Looking at the conditions of the lake, I had the urge to tell Bobby to head over to the lee shore and we would hunt the local caribou. Joe's eyes didn't give any indication of worry, so I bit my lip and we continued on. The waves were around two to three feet and starting to crest as we slid into an aptly named Banana

Bay. The long, curved inlet swept deep into the rolling hills.

As I tied the boat to a rock, Bobby was already on his way up the slope to glass the hills for caribou, puffing on a cigarette as he made his way. No sooner had we crested the top of the knoll than a white wolf made an appearance in the small valley below us. He hunted slowly across the tundra, keeping an eye out on the strange band of two-legged animals on the hill. We glassed for a half hour when Bobby decided it was time to go back across the lake.

"No caribou here. We go to other side. Lots of caribou!"

"Are you sure? We just got here, and the lake looks a little wild to cross right now," I said. All I could see were white caps and wind-driven waves, building higher and higher.

"No problem. Good boat," Bobby blurted out with a smile.

Back we motored...more like surfing down the face of six-foot waves. I just knew we would never make it across without going for a swim. But Bobby read each wave with the perfection of one who had done it a thousand times. Actually, it was rather fun, but I still had bad thoughts of sinking to the bottom of the lake with all my heavy wool clothes dragging me down.

We had no sooner pulled the boat into another small bay than I glanced up the hill and saw three bulls standing about a hundred yards away staring down at us. In less time than it takes to say it, Joe and I had our bows strung and were working our way through the boulders, trying to find a path where we could slip up on the bulls. Keeping an eye on the tops of the bulls' antlers, I moved in and out of the rocks until I was within a few yards of the last spot I had seen them. Nocking an arrow, I caught my breath and slowly peeked around the last boulder. Nothing. I looked around the entire flat of the hill. Still, nothing. Then up on the ridge, about 200 yards away, there they were, looking back below me and moving over the top of the ridge. I turned around and there was Bobby, smoking a cigarette standing about ten yards behind me.

"Did you shoot?"

"Bobby, I need to get within 20 yards of these critters!" I said. "You need to stay back and out of sight while I'm making the stalk." I glanced over at Joe and he was shaking his head.

"Can you shoot them from here," he asked, nodding at the bulls disappearing over the ridge. Obviously, I needed to do a little coaching, here. He had never guided a bowhunter before, much less one who needs to get within 20 yards. Maybe the cigarettes. Hmmmm.

All of a sudden Morris, who was guiding Jay St. Charles and Jack Joseph, came over the VHF radio. Jack was having a heart attack and Jay was giving him CPR. A Band-Aid crew from the diamond mine 80 miles away were on their way with two helicopters and Emergency Medical Technicians. We were helplessly too far away to get to Jack and Jay before the choppers arrived. Joe and I just sat glued to the radio, waiting for more information. Before we knew it, the medical team had flown in a seaplane and had Jack on his way to Yellowknife.

The day was shot for Joe and me. We glassed a little and then called it quits. The caribou could wait until tomorrow. We had to get back to camp and find out what had happened to Jack. The waves were more serene now, and the trip back to camp was quiet.

Jack didn't make it. He had died enroute to Yellowknife. According to Jay, he and Jack had spotted a small group of caribou and had made a stalk on them. Jay stayed back about 20 yards and Jack made the final stalk. As the caribou walked by in front of him, Jack drew his Osage bow and loosed the shaft. He moved a little to one side, scanning the terrain in front of him and nocked another arrow. As he began to draw, he just moaned and folded up. Jay was right on him, immediately administering CPR. He worked on Jack for the entire 30 to 40 minutes that it took to get help. Considering the desolate area they were in, the medical crew made a valiant effort to get to Jack as fast as they could. Nothing else could have been done.

Jack had hunted here the year before and had taken some nice caribou. He was so excited about this hunt that he acted like a child waiting for Christmas morning all the way up here. If it had been my time to go, I wouldn't have wanted a better time or place to be.

The bright spot of the day was that Max Thomas had been the first of the group to kill a caribou, and we ate caribou steaks and fresh trout for dinner.

That night we had a wake for Jack and toasted to his good spirit, the hunts and the friendships he had made. Billy Ellis made a speech, telling us life goes on and Jack would not want this tragedy to ruin the trip. A few bottles of good ol' Jack Daniels and we sent our friend off to better hunting grounds. My first caribou would be for Jack, I thought.

The next morning we were back on the ridge where we had seen the bulls the day before. Taking a spot behind a large boulder on the ridge, Joe and I began to glass several caribou making their way along the many lakes that make up the Northwest Territories. It was a beautiful day, the sun shining and warming up the ground. Slowly, more and more caribou came out of the rolling, rock-strewn hills.

A small group of bulls were making their way down a ridge in front of us and Joe and I decided to make a stalk and try and cut them off. I turned to Bobby and reached into my fannypack. A pack of Marlboros and a plan came out.

"Bobby, I want you to stay here. Do not move until I wave at you. We're going to crawl down to those rocks by the lake and wait for that group of caribou to come by. Here, smoke these." You should have seen his eyes when I handed him the cigarettes. As we headed off down the hill I turned around and saw the smoke bellowing out of Bobby's mouth. With a wave and smile, we were off.

The bulls were moving steadily down the ridge, heading for a funnel between the next ridge and the lake. We made it to the rocks we had previously set as our target, but the bulls were moving lower towards the lake. Joe took off well below me as I sat pondering what to do next. Turning around, I half expected to see Bobby standing behind me. But the smoke was still coming from that rock up the hill where we had left him.

I started to cross a small patch of grass to close the gap between Joe and me when I saw the antlers bobbing back up the hill. I was caught out in the open, and if the bull kept coming he would walk right up on me. Out of the corner of my eye I saw Joe start to draw on one of the bulls I couldn't see. But the caribou in front of me kept coming. At the last minute he turned sideways and put his head down. I looked at Joe. He had a bead on one. I drew and shot in one fluid motion, watching the orange shaft streak towards the feeding bull. At the shot the three bulls were off, one of them with an orange shaft stuck in him. Off he went, heading for the lake while the other bulls ran back up the ridge from where they had come.

I glanced at Joe and he shook his head. He walked back over to me and said he overshot the big bull, but he did see me hit the other one.

This one's for Jack

We waited a few minutes and then I remembered Bobby. I turned and looked back up the hill. He was still sitting next to that rock, smoking like a fiend.

"Boy, we better make sure the supply of smokes last all week!" Joe said sarcastically as he waved for Bobby to come down.

The bull had been hit in the liver and was lying by the lake. I slowly moved in and put another arrow through both lungs and he dove into the water. A strong wind was blowing and pushed him back to shore.

"This one's for Jack," Joe said. I agreed.

It's amazing how fast the guides can butcher a caribou with only a tempered steel knife and file. Bobby had the caribou caped, skinned, quartered and ready for the boat in less than 30 minutes. He was also extremely happy that the bull had died so close to the lake. We would be able to bring the boat right up to the caribou, saving many miles of packing.

Back up at the "spotting rock," as we were now calling our buffer on the hill, we began to spot more caribou moving around the valleys and hills. The sun soon disappeared and then came rain, snow and hail. It was getting pretty miserable and late in the afternoon when Joe spotted another band of bulls moving back across a large expanse of flat tundra. There was only a small bunch of spruce trees in the entire valley, but it looked like a chance to make a stalk if we could use them as a screen to get close to the bulls.

By the time we made the patch of spruce, the four bulls were feeding up to the other side. The plan had worked perfectly. Joe decided to take one side and I the other, trying as best we could to sneak through the trees. As I crawled through I kept an eye on Joe and the racks. The biggest bull was making his way straight to Joe, who was hiding beside a small rock. Lowering down, I crawled up through the short brush until I could hear the clicking of caribou ankles...a strange sound. The excitement was too much, and I just had to look up over the brush. There, not ten yards in front of me, was a beautiful bull feeding on the low grass. I lowered my head and looked over at Joe. I really wanted him to get a shot, but he shook his head and motioning that the big bull had moved out of range. He lifted his bow, gesturing to me to shoot. Nocking an arrow, I looked over the grass. The bull was now broadside with his head down to the ground feeding. Back to Joe...his eyes were wide and he was smiling and nodding for me to shoot. Quickly I lifted my body up, canted the yew bow parallel to the ground, and loosed the arrow. All I could see were the orange feathers right behind the caribou's shoulder.

He made a mad dash into the small lake next to us, and started swimming towards an island in the middle. My mind quickly scanned the scenario: no boat to get to the island; the water was too cold to swim; there was a raft, but it was back at the lodge. It was not looking good. Then the bull turned around, obviously deciding he couldn't make the island. As soon as he came back out of the lake, he lay down and it was all over. I looked back around and Joe was smiling, with a thumb up.

After the usual backslapping and photo session, Bobby made quick work of the bull. In no time at all he had caped, skinned and boned out the meat and then proceeded to wrap up most of the meat in the hide. Using a small piece of rope, he sewed the hide shut and started packing the neat package back to the boat using a head strap. We left the rest of the meat in the lake, planning on coming back in the morning to get it. It would be dark by the time we got back to the lodge.

It was a beautiful day with calm waters as we loaded up the two

The second bull of the day.

caribou and made our way back to camp. I felt lucky to have been able to take two good bulls in one day. But I also felt bad that Joe didn't connect with one. We still had four more days to hunt, and Joe would get many more chances.

That evening we had a small party with Billy Ellis making an unusually good drink with southern whiskey and Tang. Many stories were told about the day's hunt, and we got a rare chance to hear Glenn St. Charles relate his excitement of the day. He and Jay had spotted a band of caribou that were bedded on a bluff next to the lake. It was the perfect setup for sneaking up on them. Morris, their guide, slowly motored the boat out in front of the caribou and killed the engine. The wind and wave action pushed the boat shoreward, bringing them just under the bluff where the caribou were bedded. They grabbed their bows and arrows and snuck up to within 25 yards of the herd. Arrows started flying, but the caribou just stood up and looked at them. Buck fever hit Glenn and Jay as each shot became more erratic than the one before. Before they knew it, all their arrows were lying out in the ground behind the caribou.

"I'll tell you, I've never been so embarrassed. I just forgot to pick a spot! I was shooting at all of them at the same time. Man, oh man, I haven't been that excited in years!" Glenn said. "I'm sure glad that the excitement and feeling of the hunt hasn't escaped me after all these years, though!" Me too, I thought as laughing and storytelling continued through the evening. It was good to be sharing camp with such great people.

The next day Joe, Bobby and I headed back to pick up the remaining meat from the caribou, and then find a bull for Joe to stalk. We motored up the lake to a place Bobby called Dolly Parton. I'm not sure why, but I guess it has to do with the way the hills look from the water. He must have a vivid imagination, as neither Joe nor I could see what was so interesting. As we made our way to shore we ran into Goo, who was guiding for Larry and Wade.

There was a large set of antlers in the front of the boat so we stopped to admire them before heading up the hill. Before long we met up with Wade and Larry and found out what happened. The bull was traveling along a ridge and dropped down into a small valley where a line of trees made for an ambush spot. The two of them took stands in the tree line and waited for the bull to come by. Larry watched as the big bull walked past him, but was too far for the shot. He sat there and watched as the bull made his way to Wade's hiding place, and Wade slipped an arrow into the bull at less than 20 yards.

The following day Bobby and I had taken the boat out to test the water and caught several six to ten pound Lake trout. About mid day, we stopped and Bobby prepared a fire and cooked one of the larger trout he had caught for lunch. I watched as he skillfully built a fire with the green willows and flayed the trout. The meat on these Lake trout is a wonderful orange, and is some of the best fish I have ever eaten. Of course, I'm sure it also had something to do with the scenery. Bobby made a pot of tea while I picked two cups of blueberries for dessert. It was a great meal.

That evening Wade brought down his second caribou. It was another beauty, with large tops and heavy beams. By now the group of 15 bowhunters had taken nine caribou. With two days of hunting left, Larry was starting to worry that he may not be able to connect. I was starting to worry, too, as this was Larry's third hunt for caribou, and he hadn't been able to kill one yet.

I spent the next day around the lodge photographing the scenery. There are two interesting rock cairns—called inukshuks—by the lodge. The Dene used to build these man-like stone caricatures to help them find their way in this vast barren land and to herd unsuspecting caribou to waiting hunters. After the hunters had killed caribou, the rest of the tribe would skin and dry the meat. While this would take a few days to accomplish, the hunters would follow the caribou as they migrated, building the inukshuks on the way so that the rest of the tribe could find them. You can still locate these old inukshuks standing in the barren tundra.

Bertha was drying meat for me in the smoker behind the kitchen, and the wonderful aroma drew me back to camp. Smoking the caribou is the best way to get your meat home. By removing the vast amount of water from the meat, you can easily pack two caribou into your luggage for the trip home, and not have to worry about it thawing and dripping all over your gear. Believe me, I've been there. And the baggage handlers and passengers don't appreciate it either. But I'll have to admit; I had Bertha freeze four roasts for me that I later cut into wonderful steaks when I got home. A bottle of good Cabernet Sauvignon and grilled caribou steaks makes for a wonderful and romantic evening in mid winter.

There was some stirring going on down by the boat dock late in the afternoon. Making my way down the trail, I ran into a couple of guides who were all excited about a big fish "the old guy caught!" Glenn had landed a 39-inch Lake trout that must have weighed over 30 pounds. The fish had pulled their boat around the lake for a half hour while Glenn fought him.

"I thought I was going pass out, he made me work so hard for him!" Glenn said as I came up to congratulate him. The trout was massive, dwarfing Glenn as he held up the fish for photos. This was what Glenn had really wanted to do. All year long he'd call me and talk about catching one of those monsters. Now he had done it, and his smile was worth a thousand words.

Joe had also taken a caribou. The St. Charles clan had decided to hunt together that day and had gone back over to the spot where Jack had passed away to see if they could find his last arrow. They had spent a good hour looking for it, hoping to find and put it into the museum in Seattle, but it was not to be found.

Glassing the area, they spotted a band of caribou feeding out across the tundra. The herd continued on while four bulls decided to bed down. Cover was sparse, but Joe and Bobby were able to crawl behind a group of large rocks. The only problem was the bulls were still 150 yards out.

"I spook for you," Bobby whispered. Joe thought this was the only way he would get a chance at one of the bulls, so Bobby took off to the other side of the herd. The large, square rock that was Joe's blind provided two sides to shoot from, depending on which way the bulls would run. As Bobby appeared on the far side of the meadow, the bulls got up and started trotting by Joe at 15 yards. As the largest bull came thundering by, Joe placed a Canadian made pine shaft and broadhead into the bull's lungs.

To top off Joe's excitement, his father and brother had witnessed the entire event through binoculars as he had arrowed his first caribou. This was the first time in 15 years that the St. Charles men had hunted together.

A few more caribou came into camp that evening, but there were several bowhunters still waiting for their chance. One day left and it would be over. And Larry still hadn't had a chance for a shot.

The final day of hunting turned out to be the most beautiful day of the trip. All week it would rain, hail, sleet or the wind would blow like there was no tomorrow. But this day was calm and sunny. I spent the day shooting different bows with the camp hand, John McKilligan, a tall, handsome man from Red Deer, Alberta. We shot different yew and Osage orange selfbows and talked about his years of working in the North Country. It's a tough land that demands a lot of someone to hew out a living in it, but John's experiences told of his love of the barren lands and the people who lived there.

It was getting late in the afternoon, and Gary Jaeb, John and me were having a cup of coffee in the kitchen when the calls started coming in. Carol Mauch had shot a caribou. Then Nathan Andersohn. I listened for Goo to call in about Larry, but the call didn't come. As the boats started to make their way back, I sat down at the boat dock watching a blazing sunset come across Mackay Lake. Two boats were still out, one with Larry and Wade, and the other with Dale and Russ. All of them except Wade had not had a shot all week and it was starting to look pretty bleak.

As a boat started to enter the bay, I saw antlers sticking out. Larry had arrowed his first caribou, and the pressure was lifted. He had made a last ditch effort on a lone bull and slipped him a Journeyman broadhead. His smile was great to see when he stepped off the boat.

Dale and Russ still hadn't called, and we started to worry about them. It was after dark and all the boats were supposed to be back by sunset. We were sitting in Billy's room drinking whiskey sours when we heard a boat making its way to shore. John loaded up the four-track and trailer and a bunch of us putted down to the boat dock. Three caribou were being unloaded when we arrived. Dale had arrowed two bulls in less than five seconds when he found himself in a herd of them. And Russ had made a long stalk at last light on a lone bull and made a perfect shot. Six bulls on the last day of the hunt. It was a great way to end the week.

Dale had made up two dozen special arrows for this hunt. Each of them was supposed to be signed by all the bowhunters and each would take home one of these commemorative arrows. They were Canadian cedar, fletched with barred turkey feathers and tipped with Journeyman broadheads. Jack had been the only one in camp who never got the chance to sign them. After dinner Gary had the guides round up some firewood—a unique feat in itself since there are no trees to speak of for about two hundred miles from the lodge. A bonfire was started and all who knew him told personal testimonies of our late friend Jack Joseph. One of the arrows was laid among the flames, sending a lasting tribute to a friend. And one of the best eulogies I have ever heard was written and read by Billy Ellis.

As I sat looking out the weathered window of the Otter, I couldn't help but feel a little depressed. It had been a fantastic week, a week spent with some of the finest men and women I have ever shared a camp with. We had a fantastic week, with the exception of missing our friend Jack. But a piece of each of us will remain in the north country of Canada. Going home is never easy, and this trip was no exception.

"Well, you think you'll ever come back?" The excitement in the cabin stirred me from my thoughts. I looked over at Glenn and he smiled back to me.

"Yeah...yeah I think so, Glenn."

Thirteen — *T.J. Conrads*
Prairie Faith

I love the high desert of the West with its sage- and rabbitbrush blanketed prairies. The smell of the prairie and the abundant wildlife there have a fond place in my heart, bringing back memories of hunting and fishing the Snake River plain of Idaho in my youth. But southeast Wyoming is a lonely place, especially when you are sitting over a water tank waiting for a pronghorn antelope to come whet its thirst. And sitting I was, on a platform six feet high on a windmill next to a stock tank with a few dozen curious bovines milling around me.

"Get out of here!" I yelled, but they just stood there and stared, rubbing against the metal frame of the windmill and stomping through the tank. The sun was rising in the east and the temperature was following right behind it. Before long I was down to my shorts staring out across the emptiest piece of real estate I had ever seen.

It's hard to have faith at such times.

I was sitting at my desk working one winter day when the UPS driver delivered a long box to my office. "Another bow," he said as I stared at the package. I hadn't ordered anything lately and wondered what was in it, until I read the return address. As I carefully opened the box, I was immediately caught in the awe of one of the most beautiful pieces of artwork I have ever seen—a Jerry Pierce Choctaw recurve, exactly my draw weight, with my name on it.

To those who knew Jerry, his bows are the most sought-after handcrafted works of art in the bowhunting world. He never sold them, but instead made each one specifically for a reason—either as a gift to someone he thought deserved one or for a donation to a bowhunting organization to use for a raffle or auction to raise money. Well, I wasn't sure I belonged to either group after reading the simple note Jerry had sent along with the bow. So I called him and offered to pay for it. He got mad and said if I sent a check, I might as well send the bow back as well. I may be foolish at times, but I'm not stupid.

Mid February found me speaking to the United Bowhunters of Missouri at their annual Festival in Columbus. Jerry was there and we spent some time talking about the bow. I couldn't talk him into taking any money for it, and I guess I hurt his feelings. Hey, I like a gift as well as the next guy but I was humbled to have been given the bow. "I'll tell you what," Jerry said. "Why don't you come hunting with me this year in Wyoming for antelope. That would be a fair price, don't you think?"

Sounded fair enough to me, until I found myself sitting on a desolate piece of the prairie with nothing but cows around me for miles later that August.

The sun was high in the sky and the temperature hovered around 90° F. as I cursed the cows and glassed the horizon. As I turned to glass to the north I spotted a black shape moving through the olive drab sagebrush. As I watched, the black became horns. Soon a buck antelope appeared a mile away and headed toward my stand. At about 300 yards he stopped to look over the cow situation and decided to bed down. Great. Here I am, down to my shorts in plain view of this buck, getting hotter by the minute and unable to move.

It was fully two hours before the cows tired of the water scene and started tromping off over the prairie to parts unknown except to them. As they slowly grew smaller in the distant plain, I turned my head around and found the pronghorn headed directly toward me. Not wanting to spook the buck, I slowly reached down and grabbed my bow that had an arrow nocked just for this situation. The buck kept coming, almost straight at me, scanning the water tank and surrounding sagebrush like a radar dish. At 20 yards he abruptly changed directions and passed by me without offering a shot. I sat there not wanting to move for fear I may scare him away, but I was also sitting facing away from the water tank where he was most likely standing.

It was quiet except for the liquid ringing of blood pumping through my ears. Ever so slowly I tried to turn my head around to see where the buck had gone. Out of the corner of my eye I saw the orange colored antelope approach the tank and start drinking. I purposely spun around on my stool, drew and released in one fluid movement toward the drinking buck not 15 yards away. There was an instant crash of wood, my bow arm jerked forward, and I heard a loud, metallic twang as the arrow penetrated into the water tank's lip about one inch below the rim. Water shot into the air and over the surprised antelope and dust was flying as I searched to see what happened, checking my prized bow for any damage. In the meantime the cotton ball tail end of the buck was a hundred yards away, leading a rising column of dust, and getting smaller every second.

Retrieving my arrow from the tank, I found a half inch slice through the galvanized steel. An inch or so higher and I would have cut through the buck's chest at heart level. But the fact I was sitting low on the platform, leaning toward the buck when I shot, caused the lower limb to hit the front brace on the platform sending the arrow low and the buck out into the prairie. As I looked off into the horizon all I could see was a trail of smoke disappearing into the sagebrush. That was dumb, I thought to myself as I climbed back onto the platform. Now I had to explain to the landowner why I poked a hole in the lip of his tank. If the prairie was desolate before, it was downright depressing now. And to make matters

My audience, the cows.

worse, the buck stopped at the edge of the horizon and started feeding before he bedded down in sight.

It was going to be a long day.

I sat there and glassed the buck for four hours in the impossibly hot sun belittling myself and wishing—no, praying—I could have the shot back. But as we all know, these are wishes that do not come true. I thought about calling it a day and heading back to camp. But I've always believed a bowhunter needs to have faith in what he or she is doing, so I tried to stay positive about the whole episode and continue my vigilance. Hey, sometimes miracles really do happen.

Late in the afternoon the buck got up and started feeding away from me. I was glad he was leaving. I needed to put closure on the terrible events of the morning, but all of a sudden he looked back toward the water tank I sat upon. I don't really know how to say this, but he had the look like he wanted to come back in. And then he was making a beeline straight toward me from over 800 yards away.

When the buck dropped into a depression to where he was out of my sight, I grabbed my bow, nocked an arrow and stood straight up on the

platform. If he was dumb enough to come back to the tank, I wasn't going to be dumb enough to replay the first shot. As unbelievable as it seems, he did exactly that—he walked straight in to the tank, facing me, came right around the side and put his head in the water. At ten yards, broadside, my arrow took him through the lungs, low in the chest, and sailed off into the sagebrush beyond. He stood there looking up like nothing happened, and then his eyes got huge and he was off like a racehorse, making S-shaped turns through the sage and finally bulldozing into the prairie for the last time.

As I walked up to the fallen antelope, I couldn't help myself from admiring his horns and hollow hair, and the color scheme of a Popsicle 50/50 bar he sported—cream and orange. I stood up and stared out over the vast nothingness of the prairie, which once again made me feel so lonely and insignificant.

Our group consisted of Jerry Pierce and myself, along with Rich Johnson, Ken Hartlein, Joe Osvath and Gordon Rule, all of them from Missouri. We had made acquaintances at the UBM Banquet earlier that spring and were now sharing an antelope camp with Clark Noble of Hunton Creek Outfitters. It was a fine group of men and a great camp.

That first evening at dinner, the stories of the day's hunt spilled out across the table as each of the bowhunters relayed their experiences with big bucks. In fact, everyone had a shot that day, but I was the only one who connected. With five days left there was no doubt more antelope would be taken. And although I had already filled my tag for the season, there were a lot of things I wanted to see.

Our camp was nestled in a draw that was surrounded with rocky hills and juniper brush. Clark had told me this was an old Indian encampment and he had found lots of artifacts, including arrowheads. The following morning I packed my camera equipment and spent the day hiking through the hills looking for artifacts and taking photos. I found an old, partially petrified buffalo horn that was wedged between some rocks along with other strange items. And on an adjacent hilltop I came across what later proved to be an old Indian camp with literally dozens of rock rings from their tipis. Chips of red flint-like rock and obsidian caught my eye as I scoured the land. I ended up shooting three rolls of slides of a cottontail that let me spend an hour within ten feet of it, and another two rolls of a flock of sage grouse that were traveling by me.

That afternoon the landowner stopped by our camp and I explained the hole in his stock tank. He wasn't concerned since it was near the rim and could be fixed with a simple bolt and washer. Besides, he said, he wanted the antelope thinned out.

Joe came back to camp with a fine buck antelope later in the day. His first shot had hit the buck high in the neck after having the same problem I did; his lower limb of his longbow hit the floor of his platform and sent the arrow on an erratic flight. After watching the buck for some time until it bedded down, Joe stalked up and slipped it a Snuffer to put it down for good.

In the meantime, Jerry was sitting in a ground blind a few miles from camp when a herd of cattle came in to water. Two bulls got into a scuffle and started banging into the blind he was sitting in making him worry they might knock it down. A cow stuck her head through one of the shooting windows and scared Jerry so bad he punched her in the nose. She let out a bellow and roared through the herd. All of a sudden the biggest bull came over to see what was going on and proceeded to get involved in a shoving match with the other two bulls. When they careened into the blind again, Jerry had had enough and jumped up and yelled at the bulls and headed back to camp. He was quite excited when he came walking into camp that evening and said, "I'm not afraid to say I was scared. I thought they were going to roll over me out there!"

The following day was my last in camp. I had wanted to see Jerry take an antelope before I left so we discussed his options and he decided to sit the windmill I shot my buck from. Late that afternoon a buck made its way toward him and he nocked an arrow. As the buck closed in, a swarm of flying ants came through and Jerry soon had the insects crawling over his face and arms. But when they crawled into his shirt and pants and started biting him, he drew back his bow and let loose the arrow, missing the buck high. He then proceeded to completely strip down to his shorts to remove the ants. As soon as the buck was well over the horizon the ants disappeared too, leaving Jerry alone in the windmill once again...with nothing on but his underwear!

The next day I had to leave, so I bid farewell to my friends and pulled out of camp and pointed my rig toward Montana. Driving through the sage-covered prairie, I thought back to the first day sitting in that windmill. What had seemed like a bleak attempt to outwit a crafty antelope turned into a learning experience I will never forget. I had taken a fine antelope with Jerry's bow, and he was there in camp to share the experience with me. But had I not kept my positive attitude in the windmill I might never have had the second chance at the buck.

The prairie didn't look so lonely anymore as I motored down the highway into the coming night. Sometimes it pays to have faith.

Campfire Reflections ══════════════ Fourteen
The Hair Up There

C rossing the steep, rocky ledge, I realized what I needed was actual rock climbing gear: hundreds of feet of good rope, an axe and lots of pitons. This is crazy! I said to myself. Below me the mountain dropped off for 50 to 75 vertical feet into a steep slope of volcanic scree, which descended the mountain another 1000 feet to the next drop off. In front, all I could see was a sheer rock face with very few foot- or handholds. I couldn't go back the way I came—I couldn't even turn around from where I had found myself. So I fumbled in my pack with one hand, found some rope and tied it to my longbow before lowering it down the cliff. Forty-five minutes later I was lying on the edge of the talus slope catching my breath and wondering what the hell I was doing up here all by myself hunting mountain goats.

Twenty years ago, you would be hard pressed to find the Rocky Mountain goat at the top of any hunter's list of big game animals. Not so with me. I'd had a 15-year obsession with getting the opportunity to hunt these animals. To me, the mountain goat represents one animal's complete and utter defiance of man and his ability to change the world. Not only does the mountain goat call the most rugged and inaccessible corners of western North America its home, it does so with the knowledge that very few humans will ever invade its space.

I am not particularly interested in whether or not the mountain goat is an antelope that made its way across the Bering Land Bridge over 600,000 years ago. Nor do I care that some experts consider it to be related to the goral and serow of Asia, and the chamois of Europe. No, what we call the mountain goat is truly an American animal, *Oreamnos americanus*, a hybrid and adapted over such a long period of time that I consider it to be nothing more—and nothing less—than a mountain goat. And that's just the way I want to think of them.

The places they call home are some of the most beautiful and striking pinnacles of the mountain West. Just being in goat country can make one feel free of man's carnage of the wild spaces, and there are very few places left that will humble you so fast as goat country, which are some of the reasons I wanted to hunt these reclusive animals for so many years.

I applied for a permit in Idaho for ten years without ever getting drawn. For the next five years I applied in my new home state of Washington. Here the odds are better to get one of these coveted permits, though not much better. So when the permit came in the mail, I was stunned. I knew I had my work cut out for me to get in shape and do more research on the area I had drawn the permit for, an area that was open for any legal hunting weapon and encompasses over 150 square miles of goat country. I would most likely be the first person to hunt this unit for goats with a bow. This, I was sure, would be a once-in-a-lifetime opportunity for me.

My friend Jay St. Charles had told me many years before that while hunting mule deer in this area he had seen what his experience told him were some of the largest specimens of mountain goat he had ever encountered. The terrain is tough, but accessible and huntable, he recounted. So we got together and he pointed out all the places he had seen goats over the three years he had been in there. I asked if it was too steep to backpack into the area, since where I needed to be was 12 miles in and would take me up to 8000 feet to base camp.

"It's steep, and lots of rocks. You don't want to fall," he said. This would prove to be one of the best understatements I ever heard.

Early in the summer my son and I hiked up and did some scouting. We didn't see any goats, but we did find a lot of goat tracks and droppings. After returning and doing more research with Jay I decided to come in a different way, one which required me to climb 3,500 feet in less than a mile, straight up a mountain.

I spent the early part of September hunting elk in Idaho with my partner Nick Nydegger. He had made me a special longbow for my goat hunt out of Osage orange and ebony, a striking combination, and I was hoping he could come join me. Because of work commitments he was unable to. But since he had hunted goats in Idaho before, I thought I'd pick his brain a little about what to expect.

Steep country, rugged hills, scary situations...I knew that already, but cast those thoughts aside. "I'd like to go with you," he said. "What kind of food are you taking?"

"All freeze-dried, along with some instant soup and jerky," I replied.

"You'll lose some weight," he said dryly as he turned and went back to the tent. I knew that, too, but I needed to lose some weight. Little did I know I'd lose almost two inches around my waist and that my pants would fall down without a belt when I returned home.

"Take lots of rope, good rope, not that cheap stuff," he added. And I did, another thing that would prove to be not only invaluable, but life-saving as well. "What boots are you taking?"

"These Danner's. I bought them eight years ago in anticipation for this hunt," I replied. And I had, it's just that I had used them for almost all my hunting and they had been to Alaska and Canada twice and never failed me. But they were getting worn out and I was questioning their longevity.

"You'll go through them fast on this hunt," Nick said. And his comment proved right, again, as they finally gave up the ghost on my first excursion into the goat area.

Mid September found me hiking up a canyon four miles before I had to leave the trail and blaze my way up the steep mountain. It took me two days to get up to where I would base my camp. I spent three days looking over the country and only saw nine goats on another mountain five miles away. Not too much of a problem, but it was 4,000 feet down one mountain, across three miles of timbered valley, and another 4,500 up the other mountain. There was no way I could get over there and back in one day, and I didn't want to move my base camp that far knowing I had to come back this way.

After going over all my topo maps, I decided to leave and head home. I had found another way in from the east that would put me in a saddle between two ridges where I was seeing goats. And I could make use of a cow trail most of the way in. Packing up camp, I made my way down the treacherous talus mountain toward my truck in the valley below. By the time I hit the trail, my boots were tearing at the seams and leaking water. I would need to order a new pair, along with some heavy weight Thermax underwear before I returned.

Eight days later I left my Jeep at a trailhead and started hiking back into the area from the opposite direction. Although it was much farther, having access to a trail for ten miles would be easier than climbing that mountain of scree and rock again. And I had enough food and gear to last 12 days in the wilderness.

All the way in it snowed and fog made visibility less than a hundred feet. Six hours later I was closing in on my first night's campsite when all of a sudden two cowboys on horses appeared through the fog. Looking at my backpack loaded down with gear and the longbow at my side, one of them ventured a guess.

"Howdy. What are you hunting for, bear?" the one said.

"Mountain goats. I was one of the lucky few who drew a tag for this area," I replied, trying to sit down and take the load off my shoulders.

"Well, we're in here rounding up my cattle. My name is Claude Miller. If you see any cattle, I'd appreciate you letting me know."

I eased the pack from my back and grabbed my water bottle. I could tell from the look of these two cowboys they were thinking I was off in deep space.

"If you come by our camp up in the meadow, I'll cook you a steak tonight," Claude said. "Looks like you could use one." Can't beat that, I thought. So I made my way up into the meadow and put up my tent before dark.

Enjoying a rib eye steak, fried potatoes and corn on the cob with my newfound friends, I found out that Claude's son-in-law, Chris, had drawn a tag and had shot a goat three days before with a rifle close to where I had originally camped a week earlier. In fact, he told me some rifle hunters had shot three goats within a hundred yards of that site on opening day. No wonder I didn't see one goat in the area. I couldn't be there opening day and had come in a few days after.

Chris spends a lot of time in this part of the county running cattle and sees just about everyone who comes through. He told me that five goats had been killed in there since opening day. With only eight permits granted for a 150 to 200 square mile area, it was amazing that all of them so far had come out of the ten to twenty square mile area I had planned to hunt. At least there would only be two other hunters left besides me, and I hoped they were somewhere else.

My plans were to break camp the next day and go cross-country to the saddle where I had decided on basing my next camp. Chris came through again with the information that there was an abandoned cow trail that would take me up there, and that there was a small spring around the hill from the saddle. I had seen some cow trails before that didn't amount to much, so asked him about the condition of it.

"Good trail. Watch for cut logs, though. It's a little steep in some places, but it's better'n trail busting!" I had to take his word for it.

The next morning it started to snow again and the cowboys broke camp and left me all alone. There was no way I was going to attempt packing up to the saddle in the bad weather, so I hiked up the ridge across from camp to do some glassing. The sun started to come through a little and then it started snowing heavily with big, sticky flakes building up on the ground. By the time I got back to camp it was really coming down and I spent the rest of the day reading a pocket book while lying in my sleeping bag. So much for hunting.

The snow fell on and off for two days, so I kept close to camp and glassed the surrounding hills for goats. It was useless, though, so I spent time tossing flies to hungry brook trout in the creek by my camp, read, and slept while the storm passed through.

The following morning broke clear and crisp. Figuring I could get in a little glassing early in the day, I worked my way up a few thousand feet to the head of a draw which overlooked the area I had seen the goats the last time I was in here. Goat tracks were everywhere in the snow and mud, but four hours of glassing and working around the sharp crags produced no goats. And the view was spectacular with azure and orange skies and green and yellow hills.

Determined to find them, I decided to break camp and move to the saddle about two miles away. After studying the topo map, elevation and contour lines told me to wait until the morning to start up there. There was no way I'd make it by dark, and most likely not before midnight; I had to climb another 4,500 feet in two miles just to make the saddle. Not that hard, but the weight of my pack would slow me down considerably.

As I reached the saddle the next afternoon I saw a cluster of white spots on the mountain across from me. Goats! Lots of them, all in one herd. I dropped the backpack and fumbled around to find my binoculars to have a closer look. As the glasses settled down from my erratic breathing, I counted 21 goats in one herd feeding across a burned out area on the peak. Glancing around, I found my choice of base camps could not have been better. I was only about 300 feet below the end of the cirque where the two mountains connected. I had access to both mountains, and the water was right where Chris had told me it would be, 100 yards from my camp.

After setting up my tent and building a fire, I made a cup of coffee and sat down to glass the herd of goats before dark and make plans for the next morning. As I counted the goats again, a group of nine more came over a saddle on the peak and joined the rest. Now I had 30 of them in one group, not good for stalking close enough for a shot. That many eyes would make it difficult to close within bow range, I thought. By dark they had all moved farther down the ridge away from me.

Studying the topo map again, I decided it was still possible to make a stalk by coming around from the opposite side of the peak and taking a position on the ridge where I thought they would come through a saddle. Another restless night and I would finally have the chance to make a stalk.

Out of the corner of my eye I caught some movement. On closer examination I made out the head of a rather large blue grouse feeding in a tamarack tree up the hill from me. A well-placed Judo-tipped arrow brought the bird to bag and I roasted it over the fire, basting it with a special grouse sauce of mine made with butter, garlic, ginger, coriander and cayenne pepper. It was delicious, and saved me from eating another bag of freeze-dried gruel that I was beginning to hate. As I ate the bird I thought of my good friend Monty Moravec. He always said there was nothing as good as fresh grouse roasted over an open fire. I had to agree as I savored the tasty flesh of the bird while staring into the flames of the campfire that evening.

Early the next morning I moved up the ridge from camp to take a look on the backside. There were five goats, all of them exceptional billies, feeding on a small finger ridge. But there was no way I could get to them. The ridge was a sheer cliff on one side and a half-mile of scree on the other. And the only other access to them was coming down from above, which would require climbing gear. I had none, save for about 150 feet of climbing rope.

Glassing back toward the herd on the peak across from my camp, I found they were feeding up to the ridge toward a flat spot. If I could get above them, I could wait until one of them presented a shot. But it was a long way down a sharp ridge, and would take me many hours of being out of their eyesight just to reach that spot. And even if and when I got there I wasn't sure they would still be on the saddle.

Goats and cliffs be damned, I was going to try it anyway.

As I was rethinking my decision to go after the goats, I found myself too far along to turn back. After making the decent mentioned earlier, I inched my way along the ridge until I could go no farther. It had taken me seven hours to get from camp to this spot, and it was probably only a mile and a half as the crow flies. I stopped to catch my breath and looked over the ledge. There were goats all around below me, bedded in a riot of fall colors of yellow, orange, red and brown.

As I glassed the herd, one goat in particular caught my eye. It was a large billy, and as I watched he would occasionally get up and horn three or four of the goats away from the herd. He then walked broadside to me, but was still some 70 yards or so away. Time was not on my side. With only three hours of daylight left I had to wait until the goats moved closer. There was no way I could get off the ledge without being seen, so I was resigned to wait it out.

After about 30 minutes the herd started getting up and moving around, feeding and milling about. A nanny and kid started to climb up to where I was sitting, making me worry that I may get caught before a legal goat came within shooting range. As I studied the events unfolding in front of me the big billy came out from behind a rock about 25 yards down the mountain. The angle was extremely steep, and I nocked an arrow and promptly sent the shaft over his back about two inches. He blew off down the ridge away from me as I flopped to my seat with disgust. I hadn't taken in the fact the steep angle would require me to shoot lower; the arrow didn't even drop as I watched it sail down the mountain and vanish from sight. The orange ball just disappeared into the backdrop of the canyon below.

The herd was now moving in all directions, and I thought the day's stalk was over. I sat there evaluating my blunder when I heard rocks

plummeting down the mountain from behind me. Keeping my eye on the big billy, I nocked another arrow and peeked over the ledge to see what was making all the noise. Not 20 yards away stood a fine goat quartering away from me. I looked around to see if there were any kids, as it is so hard to tell the difference between a nanny and billy sometimes. Only the one goat stood there. The horns were long and the coat was beautiful, the wind whipping its hair like a mist surrounding it. The last thing I remember was the orange fletching of my arrow disappearing through its side, the arrow clattering down the mountain through the rock and scree, and forever from my life.

The goat jumped off the rock and started trotting around the ridge. I jumped over to another vantage point in time to see it stop and look back, and then it fell down and began sliding toward a cliff. At the last moment, the buildup of loose talus stopped the goat from going airborne off the cliff. It happened so fast I just stood there as the rest of the herd disappeared in all directions leaving me alone on the barren mountain with the goat and my thoughts.

It took about an hour to get to the goat. I had to climb back over the ridge and across a rock face, placing my longbow on rocks or ledges and then using all four of my limbs to move. It was tedious, and when I finally came around the ledge I stared in awe at the magnificent animal that lay before me. It took me many minutes just to get to it, and I didn't want this moment to ever end. I sat there for quite a while, running my fingers through its lanolin-coated hair, raising its head to look at the beard and stroke its horns, and admiring the soft cushions on its feet that enabled it to scale the steep terrain. Its hair lazily waved in the brisk mountain air. It was without a doubt the most beautiful animal I had ever seen, one I had dreamed of for over 15 years. As I was admiring the goat, I looked over the country and realized I had just begun, rather than ended, my high adventure.

Darkness was approaching as I quickly gutted the goat and tied it to a scrubby pine to keep it from sliding down and over the cliff. After securing my tag to it, I started to make my way back to camp. It was well after dark when I made it there. The freeze-dried dinner of peppered beef was welcomed this time.

The next morning I broke camp, loaded my backpack and made my way down the valley to a creek below where I had left the goat. Taking the pack frame with me I hiked up the mountain, skinned and boned the goat, and hiked back down to the creek by noon. Seven hours of cross-country hiking brought me to the horse trail. I finally made the trailhead long after the sun disappeared for the night. I was never so happy in my life to see "Little Red," my Jeep, in my flashlight beam as I turned the last corner and emerged from the forest.

It had been a long, arduous hunt, much tougher than I had imagined. But I had done it, and did so without the help or companionship of a friend. It's hard to explain to someone the plethora of feelings you get on such a sojourn; loneliness, sadness, fear, happiness, excitement and pure terror at times. But in the end they all seemed to meld into what I can only describe as the perfect hunt. There were those who said they wanted to have come with me, but something kept them back: too many commitments, too long away from home, too hard of country...I understand why, now.

I've always ranked the Rocky Mountain goat as the hardest animal to hunt for the bowhunter because of the terrain in which this animal lives. Sure, there are those people who make it look easy, and there those places that make it easy. But the excitement of packing into goat country, taking everything you need to live for a week or two on your back, is overwhelming to me.

I thought this would be a once-in-a-lifetime hunt. As I made my way home through the night I felt my attitude change. By the time I arrived home early the next morning I had made a vow to myself. No, I would have to hunt the bearded beast of the high country again. I could never say I had enough of it. I will never shake the feelings I experienced alone in the wilderness. I will go back. After all, it's not the destination in one's life that is so important; it is the journey that enriches life itself. It took me years to understand this, and I think I finally found it on the road home that night.

I've been told that sheep are hard animals to hunt, and they are now on my list of animals I would like to pursue with the longbow. But I hope I don't find them in the same rugged country where I found my goat experience. And to tell you the truth, I wouldn't want to. I like the mountain goat where it lives just fine.

Fifteen ═══════════════════ *T.J. Conrads*

Kodiak Special

Scanning through the binoculars, I was mesmerized by the brown, waving grass passing before my eyes. A flash caught my attention and I turned the glasses back to see what seemed so out of place in the brown sea of waist-high foliage. As I started to pick apart the brush, an antler tine moved up and down...then it was two, finally becoming a nicely formed rack of a mature buck walking up the valley, only the antlers being visible above the four-foot grass.

"One of you want to take the stalk? I can guide you in from here," I said to my hunting companions Roy Marlow and Andy Carpenter. We were sitting a thousand feet above the bay where our 50' boat was anchored, glassing a large, north-sweeping valley.

"I don't think you can stalk a deer in that thick stuff," Roy said.

"Go ahead, man. You spotted him," was Andy's reply.

Nice guys, I thought to myself. I offered either one of them the first stalk of the day and they turned it down. You can only be so congenial with bowhunters.

The buck was feeding through the thick grass and alder thickets in the very bottom of the valley, barely visible from high above. But the terrain looked stalkable, and the wind was cooperating like it should.

"O.K. I'm outta here!" I replied and fell off the mountain toward the unsuspecting buck. Working through the draw to the bottom, the grass and alders became an unmanageable force to reckon with. But the plan was working to perfection—I was well ahead of the buck and the wind was keeping my noise and scent to a minimum. Another 100 yards and I would be within range. A quick glance down at my feet made me wince in my shoes. There, not two feet in front of me, was the biggest pile of brown bear scat I had ever seen. The hair on the back of my neck stood on end and I found myself slowly turning in all directions looking for the beast that left its calling card. It looked like I wasn't the only hunter in the valley, and I sure didn't like sharing it with this one.

I continued my stalk, wondering if the shiny, round object I saw in the scat was a button from some poor hunter's shirt. Nah... couldn't be, I thought to myself more as a confidence builder rather than an afterthought. Besides, I had come too far to turn back now.

The grass in the bottom of the valley was dry and thick, making stalking almost impossible. I had reached a point where I couldn't go any further without the buck seeing me so I nocked an arrow and waited to see what events would unfold. Within a minute the buck came out in front of me walking broadside. As I drew down on him he turned and saw my movement just as I released. At the sound of the string he dropped down to gather his legs and I watched as the arrow sailed over his back a mere inch or two. With two bounding leaps he was gone.

I quickly took up his trail and soon saw his rump going through the tall grass. Keeping him in sight, I followed down the path he was on, stopping every time he looked back, until he broke from the trail at a creek and disappeared into the tag alders. Crossing the creek to get the wind back in my favor, I skirted along the edge of the water peering into the opening of the alders hoping to see where he had gone.

I had just about come to the end of the creek where it flowed into a larger stream when I saw the familiar white throat patch of a blacktail buck. He was standing on the other side of the creek looking at me. It seemed like several minutes before he turned sideways to look back up the hill, and that's when I came to full draw and let the arrow fly, taking him through the liver as he turned to leave. With a bound he disappeared through the thicket and I waited a few minutes to let the broadhead do its work.

A short blood trail and I found him 60 yards away, stone cold dead, lying in the middle of the stream. I jumped into the water and pulled him back onto the bank, admiring the wonderful set of antlers he sported and the delicate hair of his winter coat. It was just about then I remembered the bear scat and my mind began racing as to how to get the buck back to the boat as soon as possible. With the smell of fresh blood in the wind, I knew I could expect a visit from a bear if it should come across the scent. I didn't want to fight a bear for the deer, and I sure didn't want to give it to one either.

I glanced up where I had left Roy and Andy and found them already on their way down the hill. They had watched the whole episode through binoculars and were soon helping me cape and bone out the meat. It was a great first day of bowhunting.

Alaska may be the last true bowhunting frontier in North America. With so much land and so many species to hunt, Alaska beckons bowhunters from all over the world. And I've been one of them, hunting and fishing from above the Arctic Circle to Prince of Wales Island, the interior to the Alaskan Peninsula. I've spent enough time in the back country of this state that I don't feel like a cheechako anymore, although I hold no illusions to the dangers of Alaska with its unpredictable weather, bears and rough terrain.

Most bowhunters come to Alaska searching for wide racked moose or nomadic caribou, both exceptional quarry in their own rights. But our small group had come to match wits with the Sitka blacktail, a distant cousin of the mule deer.

The idea of hunting Sitka blacktail deer had been in the back of my mind for years, but the thought of packing a ton of gear, hiring a bush pilot to drop me off on some barren coast, to return—hopefully—on a specified date to pick me up, didn't sit well in my mind. But when I met Roark Brown and Rick Swenson, owners of Homer Ocean Charters, earlier in the spring, they promised me the hunt of a lifetime—fly down to the chartered boat which was anchored in a southern bay, hunt from the boat for a week while we sailed back up the east side of Kodiak Island, and all the crab I could eat. The offer was too good to pass up, so I gathered a group of six friends and we made our way north from the lower forty-eight.

The next day I spent on the boat caping out the deer head and watching Rocky Holpainen fish for true cod. He had dislocated his shoulder the first day we arrived, ruining his chances for hunting, but his spirit was admirable considering the predicament he had found himself in. So fishing was in order, and he was bringing in some impressive cod as I sat on the fantail of the boat working on the deer.

The following morning we pulled up the crab pots and made our way out of the bay toward the cannery at Akhiok. The pots produced a large king and several tanner crabs for dinner. And the ride out through the inlet at high tide took us through more flocks of ducks than I've seen

since the Pacific Flyway was at its peak in the early '80s. Literally thousands of sea birds crossed our bow: bizarre colored harlequins; greater scaup; common scoter; oldsquaw, as well as other more common species. For a half hour the birds darkened the sky as we made our way out through the narrows.

We anchored once we passed the narrows and went ashore to hunt. The low grassy shoreline held numerous deer. Closer to the hills the bigger bucks could be found, but in spite of several close encounters the only deer to fall to an arrow was a lone doe that Nathan Andersohn shot. That evening we spent the night at the cannery in Akhiok and feasted on steak, crab and adult beverages. Tomorrow we would head north, up the eastern shore of Kodiak to hunt in another bay.

The trip up the coast was fantastic. The peaks of the hills had a dusting of snow on them and the water was an unbelievable blue as the sun broadcast its warmth across the sky. We sailed for four hours and pulled into a long, narrow bay where we would hunt for a couple of days. Andy, Roy and I went off in one direction and Nathan and Greg another. Rocky remained in the boat since he was not comfortable with the idea of climbing the slippery hills with a bad shoulder.

Andy and I split up from Roy and hunted up a small hill. I dropped off one side and he took the other, where he came across a large doe feeding in an alder thicket and sent an arrow through her. It was thick and took us over twenty minutes to find the deer, although it only went 50 yards through the brush. I have to add here that this was Andy's first big game kill with his longbow. He had decided to switch from a compound that spring, and had made the decision to only hunt with the longbow on this trip. You could feel his excitement as we pulled the deer to the top of a rise to field dress it before dragging it back to shore.

The next morning there were over a dozen mountain goats feeding on the rocky cliff above the boat, some of them exceptional billies. However, because of a strong outfitters and guides association, and poor politics, Alaska law no longer allows nonresidents the opportunity to hunt these beautiful creatures without hiring an Alaska guide. So we watched them over breakfast and then went hunting after the deer.

It was a great day, in fact the best one we had had so far. In this bay, tucked away from almost every other hunter, we saw hundreds of deer, dozens of them big bucks with four and five points per side. Everyone had shooting that day, but only Nathan would connect. Late in the afternoon he had shot a fine buck, only to have nightfall approach too soon. He and Greg spent hours in the dark boning and then packing the buck back down to the shore where they could be picked up. It was harrowing at times, and they had to cross a swollen creek in the dark, soaking them to the skin in the frigid water. Back on the Sourdough, the wind was picking up as we all watched the black shoreline, waiting for a light to signal us where they were. When it finally came there was a great sigh of relief, and soon the two cold, but happy, hunters were back on board.

The weather report that evening was not good. High winds were predicted the next morning and were expected to last for some time. With only one day left to hunt, we decided it would be best to try and get back into Kodiak the next day, rather than being stuck in the bay. Although nobody was eager to leave this wonderful bay, common sense prevailed. However, we should have stayed.

Roark had the Sourdough's twin diesels fired up at 5:00 a.m. and pointed the bow east as he set a course for the Pacific. As we cleared the bay and turned north, the weather looked fine. But we had over seven hours of hard sailing to make the buoy, which marks the channel of Chiniak Bay, and a clear run to Kodiak. The ride was pleasant as we used all the inside passages working our way north.

As we approached the Chiniak Point, the weather turned foul. Ten-foot seas beat and battered us as Roark tried to slip the Sourdough through the troughs. Within sight of the buoy, he made a command decision; we could not make the harbor in these seas. So, within sight of Kodiak, we had to turn the boat around and head 18 miles south to find refuge in a safe bay for the next two days. This in itself would not have been too much of a problem, except that we were now anchored in a unit that was closed for hunting.

"You know, this is a true-life Fred Bear adventure," Rocky quipped as we sat around the dining table that evening. And it was. We had flown a Goose down the full length of Kodiak Island, taking in some of the most beautiful scenery I've ever seen, hunted out of a 50' fishing vessel, ate all the crab we wanted, fished, and now, within reach of port, we were to feel Mother Nature one more time as she taught us a little bit more respect for her power. These are things that make life so much more rewarding, and we had had our fair share on this trip.

There were no complaints coming from this quarter.

I once read that there is one brown bear for every square mile of Kodiak Island, and by my math this adds up to approximately 3,000 of these large carnivores. Their sign was everywhere, but in the week we hunted the entire east side of the island we never saw a single bear. That is not all too bad in my book—the week after we got back a local hunter was nearly killed in a brown bear mauling in the exact area we had been hunting.

The wind finally died down and we made safe harbor in Kodiak only one day late, but still in time to catch a plane back to Anchorage that evening. In the hustle and bustle of packing gear, meat and antlers, I took time to rehash the week's events. There was frozen seawater on the entire boat, and snow covered the dock as we disembarked. I looked at Roark, who was smiling the whole time, and asked him, "Well, what do have planned for next year?"

"Why don't you come back next year, but we'll just stay in the bay? I'll give you my 'Kodiak Special'! "

I thought long and hard about the offer. The decision was easy.

"I'll take it."

Campfire Reflections ══════════════ **Sixteen**

Nikabuna Nirvana

It was well past last light as I lay in my tent, the wind blowing so loud I couldn't even think. The tent poles were bent so much from the hurricane-level winds that the nylon would hit me as I lay in my sleeping bag, water rushing underneath the tent, trying to get some sleep. I had long given up the idea of trying to read a pocketbook with my candle lantern flying all over the tent, seemingly itching to pick a fight with the thin membrane that kept me and the elements from sharing the same space. So in the darkness, I listened and waited, wondering if this hell would ever end.

"Dude," Nick yelled at me from the next tent, "is it windy enough for you?"

"It's a damn windstorm!" I yelled back over the howling. "I'll fix that! Earplugs!"

What a hell of a way to start a nine-day Alaska hunt. Two days earlier, Larry Fischer and I had flown over the Nikabuna Lakes region looking for a good place to hunt. Approaching the largest of the three lakes, several caribou were seen moving through the stunted spruce.

"Look down there! A moose," Larry yelled to me over the drone of the Beaver. I tapped Tim LaPorte, our pilot, and had him circle around. When we passed over what Larry thought was a moose, I looked squarely down on the largest black bear I had ever seen.

"This looks good. Set us down and then you can fly in the other two fellas before the weather turns worse," I said to Tim. He dropped flaps, feathered the prop, and we slid onto Nikabuna Lake, which was as soft as a pillow and smooth as silk...a facade as we would find out soon enough. We found the highest ground we could and unloaded our gear. Tim would fly back to Illiamna and pick up our other hunters, Nick Nydegger and Rod Bremer.

Finding a dry place to pitch a tent, much less three, was impossible. The entire hill was several feet deep with moss, lichens, blueberry bushes and scrub spruce, under which ran a constant stream of water. By last light we had three tents pitched, all of which had to be tethered to scrub spruce and blueberry bushes, and had tied up a tarp to cover a makeshift kitchen/dining/sitting area.

I sent Larry and Rod down to the lake with my brand new First Need water filter to get us some cooking water while Nick and I started dinner. The lake was the color of mud, along the shore of which were several skulls of pike. The filter would be needed just in case there was something amiss in the water. When the boys got down to the lake, Larry promptly placed the hose in the mud and jammed the filter in two pumps. Not having a pre-filter was obviously a problem, but try as I might, I could not get the filter to back flush, making it totally inoperable.

With little options for safe water, the cleanest we could find was from the constant run off from the hill into the lake...through what I considered to be a beaver slide! The color of tea, it was palatable and so we secured it for our drinking and cooking water. Time would tell if we caught giardia...only nine more days until we get back to civilization, I thought.

Rain drizzled all night, and early the following morning we dressed in our rain gear and hip waders and sallied forth into the Alaska wilderness, pioneers of sorts as this hunt was planned around a map through the past winter, along with several phone calls to Fish & Game Officers and bush pilots. In the end, we found ourselves 90 miles from any civilization, alone and loving it...at least for now.

It was our first day of hunting and by late afternoon the wind picked up along with rain and sleet that ran parallel to the ground, eventually getting so bad that we had to spend two days in our tents. Nick was a champ the entire time, braving the weather long enough to make coffee and bring me a cup now and then...Nikabuna Coffee, he called it, with a huge tablespoon of hot chocolate and a dash of whiskey at times. After reading everything I brought, and everybody else's books, as well as the entire contents of my wallet, there was nothing left to do but sleep and wait for the storm to blow through.

This was my second trip to Alaska. Two years earlier I went on an outfitted drop hunt for caribou with an acquaintance from our local archery club and two of his buddies from his church. When we were dropped off on the sandbar that was supposed to be camp, the tents were ripped to shreds, the stoves destroyed, and no fuel or cooking gear could be found. At least we had the foresight to bring backup gear, and I did manage to kill a very good caribou, but the entire experience was something that left a bad taste in my mouth. This time I wanted to do it better; I was looking for caribou hunting nirvana.

The previous fall I put together a plan to do a drop hunt for moose and caribou somewhere on the Alaskan peninsula. Three close friends and I spent the winter preparing for our journey north. Gear was discussed, tested and tossed until we had what we thought was the best for our circumstances. When September rolled around, we were off for Anchorage for an overnighter and then to Illiamna.

Rod was a sales rep for Kershaw at the time and secured a suite at the Clarion Hotel (today it is called the Grand Alaskan). Since this was the first trip to Alaska for Nick, Larry and Rod, well, being the experienced traveler that I was, I had the hotel taxi take us down to the Great

Alaskan Bush Company...called a Gentlemen's' Club in some circles. That evening would be remembered all nine days in the bush...and today as well....

The first day we saw a few caribou, but the distance between them and us was too far; by the time we had fought our way across several miles of tundra, the caribou were long gone and we were dog tired. The tundra and muskeg was so prevalent that we had to wear hip waders all the time—even in camp where with every step your foot would sink several inches as the floating morass of vegetation dipped into what felt like an underground lake.

After trudging around for a few days after the storm in the rain and tundra, and lying in a damp sleeping bag, I was beginning to feel the need for a bath. However, with no dry wood anywhere to build a fire to heat water, and saving what fuel we had for cooking, the only option left was getting into that cold lake.

"No way I'm going in!" yelled Larry when I told him what I was going to do when we got to camp.

"I'm just going to have to put up with it," said Rod.

Nick just gave me that look...he knew what was in store for him!

Camp was in sight when the coat came off. As we entered the slim cover of the tarp, I had my fannypack off and placed my bow on a cooler. I slipped into my tent, grabbed a towel and small bottle of Dr. Bonner's cinnamon castile soap, and headed to the murky waters of Nikabuna Lake.

As soon as I got to the water's edge, I quickly stripped down. I didn't want to think about the cold, and since I was already sweaty and hot from a three-mile hike, I was mentally prepared. To say the water was cold would be a grave injustice...it was absolutely freezing. My three companions stood just a few feet away, mouths agape, as I dove in. I was out just as fast, lathering away furiously, and then dove back in. It took all of about one minute. As I stood there getting the last of the soap off, a pike stuck just its head out of the water a few feet from me.

"Look at the teeth on that dude!" Nick, the Professor, blurted out.

I covered my important parts and flew out of the water, grabbing my towel and drying off as fast as I could. By the time I had my clothes back on, Nick was already removing his clothes. "It can't be that bad if you did it!" he said. Within a few minutes, all three of my hunting buddies had taken the plunge, something we only did twice more the rest of the trip....

On the fifth day the sun finally peeked from behind the bruised sky, so we decided it was camp day—time to dry out everything we owned, take stock of our supplies, wash clothes and try to find dry wood for the fire. It was a pleasant day, cool with no bugs, clear and sunny. I had just started the second pot of coffee when a Piper Cub flew over our camp and then circled and landed. When it taxied up to our camp, a short, over weight game warden hopped out from the back seat to check our licenses and see if we had any game down.

Nick was in his Bermuda shorts painted with some tropical flower pattern. I was dressed in a wool coat and underwear...with waders on, of course. The CO looked at Nick, then at my white legs, and then turned red in the face.

"Make damn sure you haul out *all* the meat! If I don't see all the rib and neck meat when you get back to town, you're gonna have to fly your asses back up here and get it, or your gonna get fined!" he snapped. A warden with an attitude...perfect. Rain and wind had been hammering us for three days, and now Mr. Happy descends to threaten us on our day off!

What an ass, I thought.

"Hey, we know the laws of salvage," Larry fired back. With Larry being a man of such size and stature, the warden eased up a bit and then asked us how we were doing, could he relay any messages...?

"Is that coffee I smell?" the little fat man said. I poured a round of coffee and we all had a few laughs talking about how he had busted all these hunters in so many different ways. Great info on how not to get in trouble around here, I chuckled to myself.

Before getting back into the Cub, the warden pitched a wad of Skoal into his mouth, looked at Nick and me once again, shook his head and spit, then jumped into the Cub and was gone. I wondered how many other people he would run into that day.

It hadn't been a half hour since the Cub left when I glanced up on the small hill we were camped against and saw a dozen or more caribou, several bulls in the bunch as well. It was like a Chinese Fire Drill. Cups went flying, clothes were either ripped off or put on, and four half-naked bowhunters took off in four directions.

I had no idea where the others were, so, still in underwear and waders, I ran up the hill—if you can call slogging in muskeg running—and started sneaking through the scrub spruce and what few willows resided there. All of a sudden a bull trotted by me. I led him through the spruce and when an opening came available I shot. The arrow zipped through him, but a little far back. He spun and ran over the hill and down into a long valley where I lost sight of him. I walked over to where he was: twelve steps, and there was my arrow in three pieces.

In the meantime Larry had missed a bull and Nick didn't even see them. The bull I had shot was trying to find a place to lie down when Rod, not knowing the situation, saw him and proceeded to chase him farther into the valley. I tried to call Rod off, but he didn't know the bull was wounded. We waited until the afternoon, and then tried in vain to find the bull.

Early the next morning I went back into the valley to search for the caribou I hit. I knew he was dead; I just didn't know where he would wind up. The others went hunting down by the Koktuli River while I hiked down into the valley.

This is like finding the proverbial needle in a haystack, I thought to myself. No blood, no trail, no real direction to follow, and nothing but several square miles of Alaska that looks like...well...all the other square miles around me!

I had just about given up by mid-afternoon and was making one final sweep in what I figured would be the most likely place for the bull to bed down. Squishing through the tundra, my eyes played games with me. Turning and looking at everything I could for almost four hours became monotonous, and then when I turned to look back once more behind me, there he was. He had crawled into a cluster of spruce and all I could see were the upper parts of his tines. I yelled so loud I had to stop and look around to make sure nobody was watching, then yelled some more. He was magnificent. The shot had taken him through the liver.

I had the caribou all quartered and back to camp by dark when Rod came roaring in saying he had just shot a monster moose.

"Where," Nick asked.

"On the river!" Rod replied.

"On the river?" I asked, looking for some verification.

"Well, not exactly...on the *other* side of the river," was his final reply.

On the *other* side...of the swollen river. Great! Now we had to hike three miles to the river, ford it, find and bone out a moose, figure a way across the river...it was going to be hell, for sure.

Early the next morning all four of us and our pack frames and knives were at the river well after first light. Once Rod showed us where the bull was, and where he was standing, it was time to figure a way across. The only possible plan was to just get in the river, so, with clothes in black plastic bags raised above our heads, we slipped into the cold, muddy water and used our bare feet to feel our way across the river.

This is where Rod and I have a disagreement. I know it was me who was the first into the river because the other three guys were arguing over the idea and just where to cross. Rod seems to think he was in the river first. I guess time sort of blurs the truth, but the bottom line is when I reached the other side, put my clothes back on, I walked up the embankment to see a huge set of moose antlers not 70 yards away in the tall grass.

"Your moose is right there, I said to Rod, who was still standing on the shore naked.

"Bullshit!" he spat at me.

"No, he's dead, right over there," I replied.

Rod hurried with dressing and ran up the embankment. There, through a path of broken trees and uprooted alders, lying in the tall grass, was half a rack of moose antler. Rod turned and gave me a bear hug. He was so happy I thought he was going to kiss me!

By late that evening we had boned out the moose and made two trips back and forth to camp. Another cold bath in the lake was in order, then dinner.

The next day a Beaver flew overhead and we waved him down, thinking it was one of Tim's pilots. We had agreed to place a blue tarp out when we had meat so that the air service would stop and haul it back to Illiamna. However, this was not one of Tim's pilots, but another bush pilot with a party of two, and he had no room for either a moose or a caribou, much less the antlers. He said he would relay the message to Tim. However, we never saw another plane until the day we were scheduled to be picked up. The two days of hurricane weather had delayed all bush flying, so every air taxi service was flying extra hours to get through the backlog of stranded hunters.

When we finally arrived back in Illiamna, we were guests at Tim LaPorte's house for dinner, a shower and a warm bed until our flight to Anchorage the following day. Tim said that we were lucky; several of his clients' tents were totally destroyed in winds that were later clocked up to 80 miles per hour. Two hunters had their tents ripped right off the floors, blown away never to be seen again. The two fellas almost died; they slept in wet sleeping bags under the tent floor, which was held up with a pack frame in the middle. That night I went to bed thankful we had bought top of the line equipment that withstood the storm. It could have been much worse.

It's been over fifteen years since this hunt took place, and above the desk in my home office are the antlers from that caribou. I have been back many times to Alaska, to hunt bear, deer and moose. However, the novelty of being dropped off for a week or two, living in a tent, has escaped me. I think I lost that idea of caribou nirvana up at Nikabuna.

Campfire Reflections ══════════════ Seventeen

Northern Exposure

I have always been amazed at the utter isolation of the far north with its hundreds of miles of pure, untouched wilderness. But the land passing below the belly of the little Cessna caught me off guard as we swept through narrow passages and around steep, rocky canyons along the Taku River from Juneau, Alaska. Several bear could be seen feeding along the river's edge, and once when I looked out the starboard window of the plane I glanced into the face of a lone Rocky Mountain goat, a billy, staring back through the Plexiglas window.

The plane traced a path through the valleys, hills and then glaciers as we soared into British Columbia. The fall colors of the boreal forest were absolutely stunning, and as we crested the last mountain, the Teslin River drainage opened up into a vast expanse of untouched wilderness the size of which few people will ever see, much less appreciate.

As our pilot, Jim Brooks, set the flaps and banked into the lake below, I glanced down and saw the object of this trip: two huge bull moose, one on each side of the lake, were taking in the mid-day sun. As we glided down toward the lake one of the bulls glanced up as the plane slid effortlessly over him at less than 50 yards, rotating the huge expanse of antler growth like a radar's sail following our every move.

I looked at Larry and grinned. If this was any indication of what the next ten days would hold, we were indeed going to have one hell of a hunt.

Earlier that spring at the Pope & Young Convention in Salt Lake City, my business and hunting partner Larry Fischer and I were talking to Rick Solmonson and Pete McKeen of Teslin River Outfitters. They said there were two slots left for a fall moose hunt and would make us a deal if we were interested. After looking through Rick's photo album of huge moose, excellent camp, past references, and downing a few whiskeys, it was a done deal; Larry and I locked the trip up for the first ten days of October.

Little did anybody know that all our lives would be changed forever by the events of September 11, 2001. Like every other person in the modern world, I sat and stared in disbelief at the television that morning, wondering where we go from here as a human race. In the days following the cowardly attacks on innocent men, women and children, I figured our moose hunt would be canceled due to no flights in and out of the country.

Wein Air, the local air taxi service that was scheduled to fly us from Juneau to Disella Lake in British Columbia, was not authorized to cross the border. But as luck would have it, for some reason that I still do not understand, a Canadian pilot from Atlin, British Columbia, was the only person authorized to fly between the two countries in his private Cessna. After verifying the arrangements, Larry and I flew to Juneau and settled into our motel room in typical Alaska weather: drizzling rain and cold weather.

That night as I lay in bed I mentally checked my gear list. Just as I was about to fall off to sleep I bolted straight up in my bed, looked over at Larry, and told him I forgot my bow quiver. It may seem like an insignificant thing, but I thought about how I was to carry my arrows around for ten days and there really wasn't any other logical means. We discussed my options: there was a bow shop in town, but did they carry quivers for traditional bows? No telling until the morning, so there was nothing left to do but get some sleep.

Early the next morning I phoned my office and got the phone numbers of a few subscribers who lived in Juneau. An early morning call to someone I already knew, Jim Moore, and a Great Northern bow quiver was delivered to our room. Jim was a good sport about the whole thing, and I felt rather foolish to have forgotten such an important item. But in the confusion of the past few weeks it seemed almost forgivable. A well-deserved thanks, a promise of dinner on our return, and Jim was on his way. Shortly after he left the phone rang and I was told to get our gear together for the flight into camp; our pilot was waiting at the float dock to take us to Disella Lake.

Even though there were two legal bulls lying at both ends of the lake, Canadian law prevented us from hunting for at least six hours after landing in an aircraft. So after settling into our cabin, seeing off the previous hunter, and reaffirming our friendship with our guide Pete McKeen, there was nothing left to do but get our hunting gear ready and offer a few flies to the local rainbow population.

Larry hooked several huge trout, some of them close to 18 inches in length, on spinning gear as I struggled to find a fly they would take. Unfortunately, I was under the impression that the lake would have grayling and Lake trout, so I fumbled through the fly box until I glanced upon some Skykomish Sunrise that I tied for steelhead. They worked, and soon I was landing more trout than we could eat. The fishing was outstanding and by mid-afternoon we were spent and ready to head out in search of moose.

Our afternoon was interrupted when a plane chartered by the new owner of Cassiar Stone Outfitters, Greg Fournier, dropped off another guide. According to Greg, he had a rifle hunter who was coming the following day who had issues, specifically heart issues—a quadruple heart bypass, to be sure— and needed to be where he could be taken out in a hurry if necessary. This didn't set well as we were guaranteed that only the three of us—Larry, Pete and myself—would be in camp for the entire ten days. Greg left an Iridium satellite telephone and said he was sorry, but he had no choice; the hunter would be in tomorrow. This took the steam out of our evening hunt.

The next day dawned clear and Larry, Pete and I headed out in the boat to try and locate a bull. The day was warm and by noon we were starting to nod so we headed back to camp and were greeted by our new camp guest. Butch was his name, and he told us how he had never been on an airplane before, much less ever traveled out of his home state of Virginia. We spent most of the day getting to know each other. Butch related all of his past hunting experiences—of which there were around a dozen bear hunts, several trips to hunt mule deer out West, and even mention of some plane trips. By that afternoon it had become apparent that Butch was a pathological liar.

I had just lifted the tip of my fly rod, hooking another trout, when I spotted a cow moose emerge from the trees on the other side of a creek near our camp. Within a short time a young calf came out as well and the two of them fed in the tall willows. As soon as I landed and released the fish I walked back to the cook shack and ran into Pete. He told me to keep an eye out for a bull as he finished some camp chores so I sat and glassed the spruce forest hoping to glimpse a rack of antlers.

Back in the cook shack, according to Henry, Butch had looked out the window and seen the cow. He grabbed his gun and chambered a shell as he yelled out that a moose was outside. Henry had to grab his gun and tell him it was a cow and that he couldn't shoot it.

I had gone into my cabin and was stoking the wood stove while Larry worked on his gear when Pete appeared at the door. A bull had emerged from the woods and was walking up toward camp. Butch, true to form, saw the bull and again grabbed his gun and chambered a round and almost shot through the window of the shack but, again, Henry jerked it out of his hands and told him that the bull was not for him to shoot, that there were two hunters in camp before him, and never load a gun in the cook shack. Pete, Larry and I discussed the situation and decided to let Butch shoot the bull. Even though it wasn't huge, it was a good sized animal. But we wanted to let Butch fill his tag and leave so we could hunt alone.

Butch, after being told we had decided he could shoot the bull if he wanted, tore out of the cabin, chambered a round, and pointed the gun at me. I swear, I thought he was going to blow my shit away as I dove behind a tree and yelled for Larry to do the same. A terrible roar erupted and I heard Pete tell Butch to shoot again. Two more shots and the bull tumbled into the tall grass around the creek.

I wasn't sure whether to congratulate Butch for taking the bull, or throttle him for pointing the gun at me. Better judgment told me to bite my tongue and stand back.

Butch was ecstatic. He told us, again, how this was a trip of a lifetime: his first plane ride, first time out of Virginia—even though he already contradicted these stories the day before— his first day in camp and a beautiful moose down. He was happy and there was nothing left to do but congratulate him and take photos. But as he was talking and deciding what to do with the big-bodied animal, I glanced up and saw a huge bull was walking by less than 50 yards from all of us. Of course, my bow was lying on my bunk in camp, as was Larry's, and the hundred yards or so it would take to retrieve them was across an open expanse of grass. But we had to try.

I duck-walked through the grass as Larry followed, eventually residing to sit still and let me go alone. Pete was cow calling to try and hold the bull until I could get to the cabin all the while running his video camera of the bull grunting. By the time I got to the cabin and grabbed my bow, the bull was slowly walking up to Larry as he tried to become one with the willows. At 20 yards, the bull turned and continued toward camp. I moved down toward the water where he was heading and set up. But the bull would have none of it and trotted across the only open path I had to shoot an arrow, then stopped about 40 yards away in amongst the willows. It was tempting, but I knew my limitations and could only sit and watch as he slowly turned and melted into the forest.

There would be more chances, I was sure. This was only the first day and we had already seen two bulls, a cow and a calf in camp.

The next few days were clear and warm, the cows stopped calling, Butch was flown out, and we never saw a moose. We spent countless hours tossing flies to hungry trout and shooting our bows.

One day Pete showed us some handmade hide stretch boards that he and Rick had retrieved from a cabin on the other side of the lake, and told us the story of how they came to be here. An American draft dodger who escaped into Canada during the Vietnam war and had been a recluse in these parts had made these boards. Michael Oros was his name, and he had built several log structures all over the Teslin drainage, running trap lines, stealing from other people's cabins, and eventually going mad.

The story Pete relayed to us was eerie enough, but we also learned that Oros at one time had lain in ambush, within one hundred yards of our camp, ready to kill the two people who originally owned the cabin we were staying in. The people who had built the cabin had flown in to replenish stock and check things out. Oros, who had already ransacked the place a few times before, was hiding across the creek in the forest, his rifle trained on the two men. He knew he could hide the bodies, but Oros couldn't decide what to do with the plane—a Beaver—so he held off, later writing in his diaries how he wanted to kill the "sneak arounds" but didn't know how to hide the plane.

Oros was delusional and thought the government was poisoning him and sending "sneak arounds," spies, he thought, to kill him. In his descent into madness, Oros killed a German trapper, Gunter Lishy, at Hustigola Lake, not twenty miles from where we were hunting. In the ensuing months and years the RCMP eventually ran into Oros and killed him in 1985, but not before he had put a bullet into the head of RCMP Constable Michael Joseph Buday. The entire story of Oros and his life has been well documented in a book by Vernon Frolick called *Descent into Madness*.

It was the morning of our fifth day; we were halfway through our hunt, and the weather was changing. The wind was blowing in from the southeast dropping the temperature, a positive sign that our luck would change. Henry, Butch's guide, was scheduled to fly out that day, so Pete, Larry and I jumped into the skiff and headed off into the lake. We hadn't covered a hundred yards when I glanced north along the lake and saw a bull. Pete killed the engine and we glassed for several minutes trying to size up the animal. It was a dandy bull and a decision was made to attempt a stalk. To get the wind in our favor we had to cross the lake and come in from behind the bull.

As we slowly motored along, another bull was seen, then another. By the time we had reached the end of the lake we had seen six bulls, five of them shooters and the last one the biggest of all. A plan was made to work on the biggest bull and if we blew it, we would work our way upwind toward the others. Pete beached the boat and we worked out to a small rise to see if we could lure the big boy in close enough to slip an arrow into him.

The setup was good, but the bull wouldn't budge; he was camped over the top of a cow that had lain down in the tall grass trying to escape his wrath. All at once the cow bolted for the timber and the bull gave chase. It was quite a sight to see that poor cow running up and down the hill, into the lake and back out, trying to ditch the obviously amorous bull. At one point I thought they would run by us, but the cow had enough of this game, dove into the lake and started to swim across. The bull, standing on the shore and moaning and grunting, finally dove in after her.

Pete went to get the boat while Larry and I watched the melodrama unfold. The cow turned back and swam along the shore in an effort to lose her antagonizer, but the bull just wouldn't give up. She came ashore and the chase was on again. When Pete came back with the boat we motored to a point where we could see the cow standing in the trees trying to catch her breath. Within a few minutes the bull slipped into the trees as well and the two moved off. We tied the boat to a stump and slowly crept along in the willows by the shore.

After two hours I came around a bush and saw the cow not 50 yards ahead, staring back at me just before she moved off. Pete and Larry went up one side of a small rise while I took the other. I could hear the bull grunting, but could not see him as I moved up to where the land ended at a point that jutted into the lake. The three of us arrived at the same place at the same time and there was the bull, walking around an island just off the point of land. A 20 yard stretch of water separated us from the island the bull was on, and he was grunting and walking all around it. As we looked off into the lake, there was the cow swimming to the other side. The bull started to jump in after her, but Pete gave his best rendition of a hot cow and the bull turned toward us.

Larry set up in a position that would have given him a shot if the moose came up the trail, and I moved into the willows behind a stand of spruce where I could cover the other side if the bull decided to come that way. Pete called and called, and several times it looked like the bull was just about to head across the lake but would turn back toward our ambush. Just when it seemed like he was never going to come in, he turned toward our position, walked across the 20 yards of water, and proceeded to destroy a small willow bush on the other side of the trees I was hiding behind. The path he chose to come through was too close to me, and I was not in a good position to shoot in the thick willow brush. As the bull came through the spruce trees he saw me squatting in the brush. He then turned toward me with those beady eyes and began closing in. I just knew I was a goner.

It is hard to appreciate the size of a full-grown moose until you find yourself looking up at one from ten feet, but that is exactly where I was. The bull made no hesitation as he walked right at me. His antler tips looked menacing. I waited for Larry to shoot, but the time had come to make a quick decision. It was the moose or me, so I drew back my bow and slowly rose on my knees hoping the bull would offer a shot before he stepped on me. The bull saw the movement and turned, giving me a quartering angle. I picked a spot behind his shoulder and turned with him as he started to spin. As the arrow left the bow willow branches blew out from my lower limb and the arrow cut across the bull's chest, taking hair from his right leg and belly as it ricocheted through the willows beyond.

At the shot the bull whirled and ran back toward the patch and stopped to look back. Without a thought I was up and had an arrow nocked as he quartered away. The arrow flew in slow motion as it arced through the air and sunk in to the feathers at the back of the rib cage, angling up toward the lungs. Within a second of the hit, I saw Larry's arrow connect low in the chest. I spun around and Larry was standing behind me in the trail. The bull jumped back into the water and ran

back to the little island and turned back again to see just what the hell was throwing things at him and I hit again with another arrow. At the last shot the bull bailed into the water and swam off toward the other shore where the cow had previously gone.

Pete ran up to edge of the water where Larry and I were standing and asked what happened. In the heat of the battle, he had ducked behind a spruce tree and continued to call, hoping to keep the bull around long enough for one of us to get an arrow into it. He knew we shot, but he hadn't seen the hits. As we relayed the events, the bull was starting to tire and my worry was that he would die in the lake and sink to the bottom. But at last he made the short span and stood on the shore, obviously in bad shape, and then simply dropped out of sight.

We sat there for half an hour watching to make sure the bull wasn't going to get up. I was kicking myself in the butt for blowing that first shot when Larry said he had also shot and missed as the bull turned. We had both shot within second of each other on the second arrow, not knowing what the other one was doing, mine hitting first and Larry's hitting a second or two after. Larry saw my arrow hit first and stood back while I sent the third arrow into the bull. All of this happened within a matter of seconds, and the three of us were giddy from the experience.

Pete and I went back for the boat, which we had left a few miles up the lake, while Larry stayed put and watched the spot where the bull fell. When we returned we slowly motored across the water and moved up to the spot where we had last seen the bull. I looked into the bushes and just caught the glimpse of antler; he was down and very much dead, hidden below the canopy of willow and scrub pines.

We had one bull down, but now we had to decide whose bull it was and who should tag it. I was willing to have Larry tag him as I still wanted to hunt. But we all agreed that the law was the animal belonged to the person who sent the first killing arrow into it. Pete opened the bull up and checked the wounds. My arrow had traveled through the liver and into the left lung. Larry's arrow, as best we could see, cut a small hole in the heart: both killing arrows. Since my arrow had entered the bull first, and it was a lethal shot, I had to tag it; I was done hunting. All that was left was to render the beast to manageable parts, get it back to camp, and then help Larry find another bull. We still had five days left, and with the weather turning like it was we had no doubt we'd find another moose.

That night Larry cooked up moose heart and potatoes for dinner, and Pete brought out his bottle of Canadian whiskey. We toasted our good fortune, the great animal we had hunted, and to friendships that would last a lifetime. Larry reloaded his quiver with fresh arrows before bed, and we went to sleep with the sound of wolves howling into a gloriously clear and starlit night sky. Tomorrow would be another adventure.

The sun rose in the eastern sky, painting an absolutely beautiful crimson shade over Gun Site Gap as I finished doing the dishes after cooking a breakfast of bacon, eggs and toast for Larry and Pete. I was paying a visit to the outhouse when I thought I heard a large limb break across the creek. Then I thought I heard a grunt in the woods beyond. I saw movement and then the paddles of a huge bull emerged on the far side of a beaver dam, and the animal grunted as it made its way toward camp.

I bolted back to the cabin, kicked the door open, and screamed at Larry. "Get your bow! A bull is coming into camp!"

"Where?" he replied as Pete looked out the window.

"Same place as the first day. Just get your bow. He's gonna come right by the cabin!" I replied.

Larry went to our shack to get his bow while Pete handed me his video camera and asked me to film while he called the bull in. As I sat and filmed I realized this was the same bull that walked through camp the first day after Butch had shot the little one. It was grunting and working its way across the beaver dam and was heading right for us. It was going to walk between the cabin and the boat.

Larry and his moose.

Larry and Pete slowly worked their way down the path toward the boat while I ran film. As they finally made the cover of a small spruce next to the trail, the bull emerged and Larry sent a shaft though its rib cage. The bull bolted into the lake and started to swim, but then turned and came ashore and lay down about hundred yards from camp. Pete and Larry studied the situation and came back to the cabin stating that it was best to let the broadhead do its job.

A few hours later we worked our way up to where the moose had bedded and were surprised to have him jump up and move off down the lake. Even though the shot was good and had penetrated to the nock, it was obvious that pushing the bull could lead to losing it, so we headed back to camp to give him more time.

It was a long day, and when the snow started to come down we decided it was time to go after the bull. Larry and I went down to the lake and Pete did a push through the timber. The bull was on its last legs, and another arrow put the bull down for good. To say Larry was elated would be an understatement. The grin on his face said it all.

As luck would have it, the bull fell and rolled into the lake. By securing the antlers with a rope, Larry and I held it fast to the side of the skiff as Pete motored back to camp. A half hour later we were pulling the big animal ashore. I was studying the antlers on Larry's moose and asked Pete if I could review his video from the first day. The bull looked very familiar, like I had seen him up close before. Sure enough, the moose that lay before us was the same bull on the video from the first day, the one that walked by all of us as we admired Butch's bull in the grass by the creek. All the points were the same. It was an eerie feeling looking in the video camera, then at the same animal lying on the ground. Deja vu.

As the Cessna soared over the hills and dropped into the Taku River drainage, my mind replayed the events of the last ten days. Being exposed to such raw, untouched wilderness left me with a peacefulness I hadn't felt in a long time. Visions of rutting moose, evening skies filled with unbelievably bright stars, and the utter silence of the far north flashed through my mind.

As we rounded a mountain top I looked out the window and there, right on the face of a rocky cliff, were a half dozen mountain goats. A few looked up as we flew by, and I wondered if any of them had ever seen a human before. In my mind I knew the answer.

Campfire Reflections ══════════════ **Eighteen**

One Day At Mackay

I had been watching the herd of five bulls move across the tundra for an hour or so. Studying them through my binoculars, one bull seemed to be much larger than the rest. They were heading toward a strip of granite rock that ran from the lake to where I was standing, about a mile or so away. The only place to conceal myself and make an approach was from within the gray boulders that separated miles of bare, rolling tundra.

My hunting companion Andy Carpenter, and our Dene Indian guide, Patrick, decided to hang tight and watch as I made my stalk. One last glance to mark my route and I slipped into the chasm of boulders and trotted away with my head held low. The plan would work, as long as I could set up where the bulls would eventually enter the rocks as they traveled along.

Within a few minutes I neared the location I had set out for and took a quick peek over the rocks. Nothing but antlers, lots of them, and they were headed in my direction. Quickly crawling the last few yards to a large rock that would hide my presence, I set up on my knees, nocked an arrow and waited for the bulls to enter the boulder field. Another quick glance around the rock and I could see the larger bull working its way toward me, bent over and grabbing at lichens and moss as it fed along.

The clicking noise of the caribous' anklebones became louder as I prepared for the group of bulls to come through the opening I was watching. As luck would have it, the larger bull stepped out less than ten yards in front of me. Just a few more steps and I would send the arrow through him.

But that is where my luck ran out.

The bull looked up and stared right at me, wondering what this heap of wool, wood and hair was doing in such a place, and then veered to my left. He moved behind the rock I was using as a shield and walked out broadside on the other side. I swung with the antlers and when the bull had cleared the rock, I came to anchor with my longbow horizontal to the ground and released.

The sickening sound of my lower limb smashing against a chunk of granite caused me to wince and jerked my bow arm left. If the sound of wood against rock wasn't enough, the sight of my arrow entering low in the bull's neck was more than enough to bring me down. At the shot, the bull jumped and trotted back into the tundra where he stood with his head down less than 100 yards away.

This was definitely not good, I thought to myself.

A quick study of the bow's limb reassured me it had survived, although missing some finish, but I now had another problem and knew I was in for a long day. I looked at my watch: 9:20 a.m., the first day of a six-day hunt and I had a wounded animal that I wanted desperately to claim. I glanced back over my shoulder and saw Andy and Patrick high on the hill glassing over the situation I had found myself in.

The other bulls moved off, but the stricken one stayed put in the open and refused to move. Within 30 minutes he bedded down and I sat back against a rock to ponder what to do next. Off in the distance lines of caribou traversed the ancient game trails as they fed around the lake, and the sun shimmered off the water like a summer day on the ocean. I glanced back and looked at the large antlers and the feathered end of my shaft and shook my head.

Indeed. It was going to be a long first day at Mackay Lake.

Caribou. Just the mention of the word brings up images of the far north, miles of sprawling tundra and wandering herds of these ancient and noble animals of the arctic. Every bowhunter who has ever dreamed of traveling north to Canada or Alaska has had visions of hunting these nomads of the north. And although I have traveled from Northern Quebec to Kotzebue, Alaska, bowhunting many species of caribou, I have always held the Central Canada Barren Ground caribou, *Rangifer taranus arcticus*, as one of the finest caribou to bowhunt.

I was hunting at Mackay Lake with Gary Jaeb of True North Safaris in what is the Northwest Territories. Gary has been outfitting and guiding for caribou on this northern lake for many years, and has one of the finest caribou operations to be found anywhere. After my initial trip here in 1993 I knew I would have to come back.

Our group this year consisted of 24 traditional bowhunters from all over the country who had gathered here to enjoy the camaraderie and excellent bowhunting that True North Safaris is known for. Situated on the shores of Mackay Lake, the lodge serves as a base of operations where bowhunters can access over 100 miles of coastline of this arctic lake. And if the excellent hunting opportunities weren't enough, Mackay Lake has some of the finest Lake trout and grayling fishing to be found anywhere.

My plans were to hunt for a large bull, one much bigger than the two previous ones I had taken from here, and then spend the rest of the week fly-fishing and taking pictures.

The first morning Andy and I left the lodge at first light with our guide, motoring an hour east on the lake before we pulled into a little harbor. Literally hundreds of caribou were working their way down the lake's edge, darkening the shallow valleys and silhouetting their beautiful headgear against the early morning sky. We had already taken a few stalks and were climbing up a long, narrow ridge so we could see more of the country and find stalkable bulls.

The day was glorious: clear blue skies, rising temperatures and a stiff wind from the west. But by 9:00 a.m., I had found myself in the situation at the start of this tale....

The bull laid there out in the open tundra for what seemed like hours. The wind was coming directly over his back toward me as he stared at the field of large boulders. He knew the source of his trouble had come from within—possibly that pile of wool that didn't belong—and kept a vigilant watch in my direction.

After an hour or so of glassing the bull I knew the shot wasn't fatal, at least anytime in the near future. I also knew I had to find a way to get close enough to put a clean arrow through him if I was going to harvest the bull. A wrong move, a whiff of my scent, or any other number of events could send him farther out into the tundra where he would never be found. So I relegated the rest of the day to try and find a way to get to him, and if it took all day, well, so be it. I owed him—and myself— nothing less.

As I glassed the immediate area around the bull, I found a slight depression that would take me close to him. I pulled my wool hat down tight and low and began a slow crawl through the rocks and out into the tundra on what I hoped would be a successful stalk. As soon as I had left the security of the rocks the bull got up and turned around. I froze in the tundra, belly down, as muskeg water seeped up through my clothes soaking me to the bone. The bull stared off into the horizon and then turned back towards me and lay down again. This plan wasn't going to work so I backed off to the security of the rocks once more.

By now the sun was near its highest point for the day, so I took off my wet clothes and made my way back toward the boat. A little lunch and a plan was what I needed. After a quick sandwich and cup of coffee, I had the plan; I was going to work my way around the shore of the lake and come in behind the bull across a mile of open tundra. The wind was strong and driving straight over the bull's back, but I knew if I came in crosswind I could get right up on him. My only concern was what would happen if he got up and moved off before I could close the distance.

No more debating. I had to make my move.

An hour later I ran into Gary Jaeb who was helping two of our group find caribou. "What are you doing up here?" he asked as I slumped to the ground in front of him.

"Sweep your glasses over that open valley and tell me what you see," I replied. He did and pulled his glasses away from his eyes and smiled at me. "No, he's bedded, and I need to finish the job. I am coming in from this angle to get the wind right and try and sneak up to him," I added.

Gary took a long look at me. I knew what his thoughts were so I shook my head and said, "Wish me luck."

"You'll get him," he said as I turned and headed off across the tundra.

It was tough. Every ten or twenty yards, the bull would move his head and I would dive into the muskeg. Although he was bedded in a depression in the tundra, I could keep an eye on him by focusing on which way his antlers moved. Even though I was wet, the sun, tension and exertion of duck walking over a mile of undulating tundra was taking its toll.

So many questions popped into my head such as: What will happen if I spook him? Where will he go? Will I get a shot and, if so, will I make it after all this? The pressure was heavy, and as the hours wore on I began to doubt my own ability to pull this stunt off. It seemed like an eternity, and I had never so deeply questioned my own capabilities as I did while I slowly crossed that open field of lichens, moss, hummocks and water.

Halfway there I shed my binoculars; I didn't need them anymore, as I knew every curve, point and protrusion on those antlers. Next went my wool shirt, as it was soaking wet from water and sweat. At 50 yards or so I dropped in behind a hummock and lay on my back starring up into the sky. Beautiful white clouds streamed by and my mind wandered to faraway places and events. I just didn't want to think of what was going to happen. I stole a quick glance at my watch; it was 1:20 p.m., a full four hours since I shot that first arrow.

It was now or never.

Rolling over I slowly raised my head over the hummock and stared at that magnificent headgear. The wind was right and the bull was facing away, so I crawled up to within 15 yards before I felt I was ready to make my move.

I rose to both knees, arrow nocked, and came to anchor just as the bull became aware of a presence that should not have been there. Before he could bolt to his feet, my arrow zipped through both lungs. He jumped up and made a dash 25 yards before stopping, legs splayed, and piling up on the tundra for the last time. It was obvious that if I had missed he would have run forever; his neck wound was nothing more than an irritation to him. But I had to finish the job and was grateful it had turned out the way it did, nevertheless.

Tears literally flowed down my cheeks as I walked up to the bull and sat down. I stared at his beautiful coat and huge antlers and thanked God for my being able to finish the job I had bungled so badly in the beginning. I don't remember much after that until I felt Andy standing by my side. He had watched the whole stalk from up on a ridge of rocks and had come running down across the valley. I never heard a thing until he touched my shoulder and said, "Nice bull."

Our group of bowhunters had succeeded in taking 21 bulls in six days, four of them the first day. And as planned, I spent the better part of the week fishing for Lake trout and grayling, exploring new waters and enjoying the fine weather we experienced. The last evening we had a big bash in camp, dancing to native Dene drums and enjoying the festivities of another hunt for the memories of time.

As I stepped outside the lodge and stared out across Mackay Lake, I couldn't help but be thankful of the final outcome of the first day. In the end I learned more about myself, the animal I was hunting, and the meaning of doing the right thing in the field.

The drum beats and singing caught my attention as the sun sank over the horizon, beckoning me to come inside and celebrate. And so I did.

I had much to celebrate about.

Campfire Reflections ══════════════ **Nineteen**

A Never Ending Journey

Bowhunting can take the hunter to some faraway places. Just getting there can be an adventure in itself.

It had been a long trip. Twenty-two hours of driving from Seattle, Washington, to Prince Rupert in western British Columbia had taken its toll on the four of us. And the 17-hour junket from there to Ketchikan and on to Prince of Wales Island on an Alaska ferry crowned our exhaustion. But it was almost over and here we were in the small town of Craig on Prince Of Wales Island in southeast Alaska. A short nap in the motel and in the morning we'd be off to the north to launch our boat for the long trip to our camp—a rented Forest Service cabin on a salt chuck.

"What'll it be, boys?" Glancing up at the lady behind the counter, I couldn't believe I was actually sitting in a real chair that was neither rumbling down a highway nor lolling in the sea. But we still had another day of traveling to get to our camp: four hours on the road, and two to three boat trips into the area we were planning to hunt in.

"A beer and a pastrami sandwich, Ma'am." Sustenance, at last.

Late the next afternoon we finally made camp at our cabin on Barnes Lake. Being a salt chuck, getting into and out of the lake from the ocean is quite a feat. The two ways into it were passable only at high tide, turning into a rushing river with huge rapids during tidal movements. It is a great experience and quite strange to see this "river" bone dry at low tide and deep and flat at high tide. With the 24-foot tidal range, you have to time your entering and exiting the lake. By the time we unloaded the gear and set up camp, it was too late to do much of anything but make a hasty dinner and retire to our sleeping bags.

Tomorrow would be a new day.

It seemed like we'd never get a chance to hunt bears.

I like hunting bears. And I never miss a chance to put my skills to the test when the opportunity presents itself. So when my friend Rocky Holpainen asked me if I would like to accompany him and a few others on a trip to Alaska, I couldn't refuse. But I never imagined that just getting there would become a trip in itself.

Since I could only get away for a few days, I planned to fly out halfway through the hunt. This worked out great since one of our group, Russ Tye, was scheduled to fly in on the same day. We would just trade places at the small airport in Craig and I'd make my way home while Russ hunted the second week.

A quick call to my hunting partner Nick Nydegger of Earth Archery in Boise, and we had a group of four to make the trip up. Nick and I would hunt for four days and then fly home. Russ would come in and hunt for the second week with Rocky and Randy Gehrke. If it sounds complicated, it was...but everything worked out all right.

Hunting bears in this part of Alaska means many hours of glassing the short, grassy areas of the tidal flats. Floating around off shore and glassing the beach is the best way to spot a bear. Once spotted, you make your way to shore where you can get out and make a stalk on the feeding bruin...if everything goes right.

Weather in southeast Alaska is unpredictable at best. Wool is the clothing of choice, under a generous layer of waterproof rain gear. However, the temperatures may also range into the high seventies, as it did the entire time I was there. Cotton pants and T-shirts come into play then. I made the mistake of not bringing a set of lightweight pants, and suffered during the middle of the days with my wools. But I wasn't about to let that bother me; it is better to be over dressed rather than under.

Early the next morning we found that the little island a hundred yards off shore was now connected to us by land—a lot of it. The tide had literally left it high and dry. Nick, Randy and I spent the morning digging up a bucket of clams for our dinner. I love seafood, and from the looks of it we were going to have our fair share.

Nick and I decided to hunt down toward the ocean, checking all the

creek mouths for bear sign, while Rocky and Randy went out in the boat to glass the shore. We saw a few bears across the lake, but because we were on foot there was no way to get to them before they disappeared into the thick jungle of rain forest.

We found numerous areas where bears had dug up the ground, but hadn't run into any of them by noon. Building a small fire on a rocky outcropping, I dug up a hat full of Pacific mussels and cockles. Nick removed a one pound coffee can from his daypack and heated up some salt water from the lake. A quick boiling of the delectable bivalves yielded a wonderful lunch while taking in the scenery.

Working our way along the shore, the tide started to change and soon the calm was replaced by water rushing down rapids toward the ocean. I looked over and spotted a bear gobbling up the grass at the mouth of a small creek pouring into the river. Belly crawling my way to within 30 yards of the bear, I eased up and looked out over the top of the grass. He was a large bear with that desirable white tab on his chest, tearing at the grass and watching the area behind me. I had penetrated his domain and he had no idea I was around.

If you've hunted bears very much, you understand the heightened sense of excitement when you find yourself within the bears' private "zone" of safety. It can be both exhilarating and scary, depending on what happens next. I should know; I've been chased up a tree by a pissed off sow and had to beat her back with my longbow. Thanks to my loud yelling and well-placed blows to the head, she yielded me a small spot of the side of a pine. And I have also been lucky enough to slip a broadhead through a large boar who never I knew I was a scant 20 feet from him when he took his last bite of spring grass.

But, for better or worse, today neither of these two scenarios would come to pass. Just as I was positioning myself for a shot should the bear turn, the wind shifted and he was gone. I stared into the rain forest, trying to will him back into the open. It was several minutes before I felt Nick standing over my back.

"What are you doing?" he said.

"He was there, wasn't he?" I replied, not really sure if I was dreaming or hunting. He was a great bear, larger than any other bear I had taken. Nick's smile was welcomed and we headed off farther down the river to the sea. It was the first day and I knew we would see more bears in the days to follow.

That night over a fine dinner of steamed clams, Randy and Rocky related their experience with a bear across the lake. This bear always came out at the same spot next to some large commercial crab pots, ate a few bites of grass, and then would slip back into the brush before they could get the boat to shore. This would be the norm over the next several days.

The following day we made a boat trip up the river to another lake, glassing and scanning the creek mouths as we went. There was lots of bear sign, but no bears. We stopped at the last big pool before entering the lake and tried our luck at fishing. The steelhead run was all but over, but we were seeing some rather large sea-run cutthroats cruising by the rocky shore. They weren't interested in my flies, which I thought was strange. I've always been able to coax a fish to take a fly if I try hard enough and give it a lot of dinner selections to look over. But today it wouldn't work.

The day was lazy, no bears were seen, and no fish would take our terrestrial presentations. Some days are like that. But I've come to appreciate the fact that nothing comes easy in the outdoors, which is one of the reasons I choose to hunt with a longbow.

The plan for the next day was to exit the salt chuck at high tide and hunt the outer coast of the island, and hopefully to make it back with the following high tide late in the day. Timing would be crucial or we would be waiting all night for another high.

The next morning I was dinking around camp, getting my gear prepared for the trip while Nick and Randy headed down the beach to get in a morning hunt. As I walked down toward the boat to start loading my gear, I glanced up the beach as I usually did and noticed something black. Now, I had seen this particular stretch of land a hundred times or more in the last few days, and that black spot was never there before. As if by magic the spot became a head, then body...a bear came out of the woods not 300 yards from me. Then there were two. I went straight to the cabin for my bow, never giving the bears a second look.

I whispered for Rocky, but he was back in the woods somewhere, doing something, and I wasn't about to wait for him before making a stalk. Past experience told me that I had a limited amount of time to get within bow range before the bears would make their way back into the forest and literally disappear. So off I ran down the beach to close the distance.

When I got to within a hundred yards I ran out of cover. They were feeding around a point with a fallen tree running out toward the shore creating a snag. The small cove in front of me opened up a wide swath for the bears to see me if I moved. So I sat and waited, glassing them as they fed around the fallen tree.

Ten minutes later the last bear hopped onto and over the tree and was gone. As quietly as possible I trotted over to just below the tree and nocked an arrow. As I was catching my breath I was mentally choosing the larger bear, if I should get a shot. Slowly stalking up to the side of the large snag, I took one last breath and eased my head and shoulders above it.

There was only one bear in sight. The other had disappeared. All of a sudden I felt that feeling I mentioned a while back about being in the zone of a bear, and this was not the exciting one. I thought that it was just on the other side of the tree, not five feet from me. With this feeling driving me, I immediately stood up all the way, coming to full draw while I feverishly glanced up and down the tree for the hidden bear. Nothing...it had totally vanished into the woods. Relieved, I looked back at the other bear and let the bow down. It saw the movement and turned its head straight at me. I froze in place waiting for the game to be played out. Would it bolt, or would we just stand there for an eternity until one of us lost his wits? The decision was made on the bear's part as it put its head down and began feeding again.

The orange fletching of my arrow vanished into the bear's side, tight behind the shoulder. I guess that's the real magic of shooting a longbow; it becomes so automatic, the mechanics involved, that your mind focuses totally on where you want the arrow to go. At least that's the way it is for me. The bear took off into the woods while I tried to mark its escape path. With the thickness of the forest, anything less than a perfect chest shot could spell disaster while tracking. But I've always made it a point to know exactly where my arrow hits an animal, and this one was nothing less than a perfect double lung shot. As I mentally marked the exit spot of the bear, it reappeared less than 20 yards away, running back to the beach before it stumbled and fell dead against a log. It was that fast, and that long.

After getting the other guys to help me drag the bear out to a rocky outcrop where I could dress and skin it, the three of them headed out into the lake to glass for more bears. I guess I kind of ruined our plans to go outside the salt chuck, but I think it was a mutual decision to stay in the lake. And they did indeed see bears, but all the stalks came to nothing.

My last day was spent fleshing out the hide and skull of the bear, while the others ran around the lake glassing for bears. That evening we were heading out and back to Craig where Nick and I would catch a plane for Ketchikan and then on to Seattle, so Nick was eager to get in a stalk before we left, and he only had a few hours to do it in.

The same bear was again out feeding by the crab pots. It was Nick's turn to take the stalk and after dropping him off well down wind, Rocky and Randy took the boat out into the lake to watch the showdown. Nick slowly made his way to within 30 yards of the bear. As the gap was being closed, the bear just blew out of the area. Nick stood up and made his

way back to shore to wait for the boat, all the while shaking his head and smiling. The story is a good one, but awfully strange.

Now, the way I am to understand this, Nick had stalked the bear as it fed down the beach for quite some distance. He was crouched behind a piece of driftwood, ready for the shot if the bear would turn away. As the bear slowly turned and approached the driftwood, a little excitement overcame Nick, and he released a little pressure. I guess what I'm trying to say is that this is the first time I've ever heard that flatulence had chased a bear away, but that's the truth. Honest. Just ask Nick.

And so ended my short trip to the southeast of Alaska. No sooner had I left than the rain started and continued until the rest of the boys left. But more stalks were to come, Rocky finally connected on a bear, and Rusty figured out what the cutthroats wanted and caught more fish than he could count.

I came home with fond memories of elusive bears, good friends and a strong, compelling urge to do it all over again. But next time, I think I'll fly up.

Ruminations

Twenty ════════════════════════════ *T.J. Conrads*

The Professor

I t's rare to find that perfect hunting partner. You know, the one you can spend time with in a wall tent or backpack tent for extended periods of time, without having the feeling you want to kill him...a friend who knows how you hunt and compliments, rather than hinders, your abilities. A partner who can cook, share camp chores, who hunts hard and ethical, and makes you laugh. I have a friend like that: Nick Nydegger, aka The Professor, better known as The Prof.

I first met the Prof twenty-something years ago. I was in the military at the time and had joined a local archery club in Boise while stationed forty miles away at Mountain Home Air Force Base. We hit it off immediately and fast became good friends. Little did I know that we would remain, and still are, close friends and hunting partners over all these years. And the times we have spent together have been interesting, informative and never dull!

Monikers are usually earned, not given. The Professor's came about during a bowhunting trip to Alaska in 1988. This was Nick's first excursion to Alaska. Along on the hunt were Larry Fischer and Rod Bremer. Our plans were to scout a few areas by airplane, find a promising location, and be dropped off for nine days of bowhunting. Our quarry was moose first, and caribou second.

Being educated in ictiology and chemistry, Nick spent most of the trip on his hands and knees, studying the lichens, moss and other biological flora instead of actually hunting. Every day we all would return to camp with stories about what was seen, stalked or missed, but Nick would elaborate on some new species of plant life. "I could spend a lifetime up here studying these plants!" he said one night.

One day Larry and I were sitting on a knob behind camp that we used as an observation point and were glassing the surrounding area when we spotted Nick working his way back toward camp. As if on cue, he looked down into the tundra, stopped, and bent down to have a closer look.

"The Professor," Larry said, and the name has stuck ever since.

Point Blank Elk

I had been hunting one of my favorite elk haunts I called The Hell Hole, and for good reason. It was a nasty hole in the side of a mountain with steep, rocky cliffs on three sides. The easiest way to access the Hole is from below, but it is heavily timbered and high up the side of the mountain, so the way I always enter it is from the top. It is hellish in that once you managed to find your way down into it, getting out is three times as hard. But the Hole holds elk.

For three weeks I had hunted what I named the Calliope Bull. This elk had a bugle that would warble through several scales, finally ending with one of the sickest grunts an elk could make. In fact, for two weeks I thought it was an inept hunter, but he was always there, day and night, singing with such an awful bugle that made me believe it had to be the real thing; no real bowhunter could sound this original, or bad.

Finally I could stand it no longer and dropped into the Hole. I ended up calling in a small spike and running an arrow through him just as the Calliope Bull came over the ridge right behind me. With my tag punched, and the big bull standing there, I had but one thing to do and that was pack the spike out of this miserable place. On returning to Boise, I managed to get the Professor to spend the last day of the season chasing the Calliope Bull.

We had no sooner got out of my truck when a fork-horn mule deer jumped up in front of me. I promptly bounced an arrow off his back and Nick laughed so hard I though he was going to pee his pants. Once he settled down we sat on the rim overlooking the Hell Hole and I gave a short bugle. Immediately the Calliope Bull shrieked back.

"That ain't no bull!" Nick spat as he turned to me.

"Dude, I've been chasing that guy for three weeks. He's there and he's real!" I shot back. I called again and the bull blasted back once more. I looked at Nick and said, "Let's go, Bud. This is your bull!"

We fell pell mell down the far side of the ridge through some of the nastiest brush I have ever seen. Not a hundred yards down I tripped and fell over a deadfall. Nick laughed and I was cussing him when I saw a cow elk lying not ten yards from him.

"Nock an arrow and shoot that cow!" I whispered.

Nick looked at the cow as she just sat there, not seeming to have a care in the world. Nick glanced at the cow and then at me, and shook his head. "Let's go find the bull." We took off and I spun around to see the cow give me a strange look. I think I must have passed as a non-threat...must have been the theatrics of tumbling over the deadfall.

We had finally closed the gap and I set up to call while Nick slipped into a stand of small pines. With one bugle the bull was standing there, right in front of me and broadside to Nick. He bellowed out his characteristic tiered shrill and then just stood there. All I heard was the metallic twang of an aluminum arrow, several feet above the elk's back, as it ricocheted through the trees. I was less than ten yards in front of the bull when I saw his eyes grow larger and larger until he finally realized something was not right in the woods. In a flash he was gone.

"I shot a foot over his back...I think! Hell, I don't know where I shot! I don't think I picked a spot!" Nick blurted out as he walked up to where I stood.

We never saw that elk again.

The Lantern From Hell

"Where's your lantern?" Nick asked me as night was descending on our mountain hunting camp.

"In the white five gallon paint bucket...wherever that is," I responded. "Where's yours?"

"I dunno, maybe in the truck. I'll go and see," he replied. He went into the back of his Ford and removed a green bucket. As soon as it was opened he smiled and pulled out a double mantle Coleman from the bucket. "Needs to be filled. Where's the fuel?"

"Want me to fill the thing?" I asked, knowing that every time he fills a stove or lantern, he has a tendency to either spill or overfill each unit.

"I got it" he replied and went about looking for his funnel.

I went to work starting dinner; fried deer back straps, baked potatoes and onions, the result of Nick having tagged a fat fork-horn the day before. I had yet to even have a shot, but hey, an animal in camp, no matter who shot it, is a good thing and we were getting ready to enjoy it.

I was slicing onions and it was getting dark. "Having a hard time with that light?" I snickered over at Nick. He was serious now, staring back with a glare.

I was just getting ready to slide the plateful of sliced onions in the cast iron skillet when I smelled gas, and lots of it. I turned to Nick and he was just getting ready to spark a match to the lantern when I said,

"I smell gas."

The flame flicked and burned like it always does before the generator gets hot enough to vaporize the fuel. Then it dropped low like it was about to go out. Nick was reaching for the fuel knob and I was just about to warn him when all of a sudden the entire lantern lit up, inside and out, along with Nick's hands. In a flash the lantern was tossed and Nick rolled his hands in the dirt, putting out the flames before I could even react. He looked straight at me...my eyes were wide open in surprise...and said, "It don't take me long to look at a lantern!"

Without saying a word, he walked into the tent and emerged with a liter of Evan Williams whiskey in one hand and my lantern in the other. Handing me the lantern, he pulled the cork from the whiskey bottle, gave me a twisted look, and tossed the cork into the fire pit. "Won't be needing that any more tonight," he dryly stated and sat down beside me.

Funny, he has never mentioned that night since....

Culinary Delights

One of the best parts of hunting with the Professor is that we both love to cook as much as we love to eat. If you have ever been lucky enough to hunt with us, then you may have experienced such gastronomical-heady meals as grouse smothered in wild mushrooms and garlic; sausage, cheese and tomato omelets with fresh melon; homemade burritos with avocado and sour cream; T.J.'s World Renowned Feathered Potatoes with three cheese topping in a Dutch oven; or fiery BBQ pork ribs with fresh corn on the cob and salad with blue cheese and fresh baked Dutch oven bread. Between both our grub boxes we can turn Spam and peas into a meal that most folks would rave over. Very little canned food in this camp, except for a few vegetables and sauces used as condiments to accent a much grander meal. However, sometimes the devil comes out and the results are, shall we say, evil!

It was a fine September day and I had just arrived from Washington and set up camp in short order for our annual elk hunt. In my larder I had several types of Seattle salami and sausages and a few new recipes to throw at Nick.

As usual in the mountains of central Idaho in September, the rain started in the middle of the day, turning to snow by late afternoon. Retiring for the day to the warmth of the wood stove in the wall tent, we popped a few beers and I started dinner. Tonight's specialty was hot Italian sausage in sauerkraut.

By the time the sausages were steamed and I added the sauerkraut and other spices to the cast iron pot, Nick pulled out a jar of jalapenos and ate a few. "Go ahead and throw some in the 'kraut," I said as I popped another beer. Tasting the delicate dish, I sensed it needed something else, so in went more jalapenos, as well as some of the liquid. A few more beers, a lot of talk and laughter, and it was time to eat.

The Professor whipping up breakfast.

With dinner ready I dished out a bowl for Nick and one for myself, then we sat back to enjoy the meal along with some fresh sourdough bread. The first taste wasn't bad, but by the time I got the second mouthful down my eyes started to water, I was gasping for breath and Nick was laughing. Reaching for my beer, I noticed the jalapeno jar was completely empty! Needless to say, Nick thought he would spice the dish up a little more as I was turned away. It was about the hottest thing I have ever eaten.

That night was miserable. I was up most the night eating Tums and drinking glass after glass of Alka Seltzer. To make matters worse, as anyone knows, the next morning as we drove to a new area to hunt, I had to stop four times and make a mad dash to the nearest tree. To say dinner burned going in and going out would be a vast understatement! And the Professor just sat there and laughed.

A Pack For All Seasons

Hunting packs are a necessary evil. I started out with a simple, small fannypack many, many years ago, and ended up working my way into a full backpack. Like all of us bowhunters, I carry way too much stuff, things that I have absolutely no use for. And the Professor is the reason for much of the clutter I now pack.

A few years back he had moved up to a rather large hunting pack, custom made, and found that it still couldn't carry enough stuff. So, he had another custom pack made—this one a fannypack—that hooked onto the bottom of his main pack. I told him he might as well just use a 7,000+ cubic centimeter pack; he just glared at me.

I used to rib him about the amount of stuff he crammed into his hunting pack, but over the years these otherwise useless items have made our hunts more enjoyable, and sometimes downright bearable.

We were hunting bear on Prince of Wales Island in Alaska and staying in a forest service cabin on the north side of the island, accessible only by boat. The lake we were on was actually a tidal lake: the saltwater rushed in and out twice a day, with tides as much as 23 feet difference between high and low.

One afternoon Nick and I were hunting out toward the ocean when we came across a huge bed of cockles, my favorite species of clams. "Oh! I wish we had a pot to cook some of these in!" I said to Nick. He looked at me for moment, winked and took his pack off. Out of one of the side pockets he pulled an empty 1-pound coffee can. I quickly started a fire in the rocks and we sat there for several hours, eating fresh steamed cockles on the beach. They were, and still are to this day, the finest tasting clams I have ever eaten.

Another time we were hunting elk in the late season when a sudden snowstorm put us under a stand of sub-alpine fir. It was cold, but the fir kept the driving wind at bay. As the snow and wind increased, I took out a space blanket and tied it to a few of the limbs to create a windbreak. Even with this added feature, in no time were both cold and starting to shiver.

Nick dug into his pack and removed a stainless steel mug, a military heat tablet and some instant soup. I grabbed a few rocks, snapped off some of the limbs around us, built a small fire and we sat there and

Campfire Reflections 153

The Professor and I discuss the culinary usefulness of a double-broadhead shot spruce grouse.

drank hot soup and coffee until the storm ebbed enough for us to get back to camp. I am not sure how the situation would have turned out without the hot liquids to keep us warm, but I do know that it was one of the best meals I have ever eaten!

I can't tell you the number of times we have been in the woods, needing some small thing or another, and it has materialized out of Nick's pack. Whether it is an extra flashlight or knife, game bag or water filter, broadhead and Judo point, or even a 16-inch piece of cord to tie a grouse to your belt, Nick always seems to have it with him.

The only thing about the Professor that bothers me—and just about everybody who knows him—is his total and complete lack of doing anything on time. All of us who know him consider it "Nick Time," which is at least two hours later than what he says, and usually a lot longer...sometimes up to two days.

It doesn't matter what it is: dinner engagements, hunting pick-up times, a meeting somewhere...he is chronically late and that is expected. As an example, if I schedule dinner at my house—less than three miles from Nick's house—at a certain time, he will be fashionably late. Always. You just have to expect that from Nick. I always figure an hour, at least.

Just this morning I called him to find out when he would be in elk camp. It was before 10:00 a.m. "I'm leaving within the hour and will be there by early afternoon, he told me. Well, I called him at 3:30 p.m. just to make sure he wasn't lying on the side of the road and he said, "I'll be there around 6:00 p.m....I'm running a little late. Well, as I write this it is now 6:30 p.m., dinner is done and getting cold, and I doubt I'll see him before dark!

The other thing that really gets to me is that 99% percent of the time he is going a million miles an hour with his hair on fire. But the moment he gets behind the wheel of his truck, it is slow motion like you have never seen! Speed Limit? Hell, that is just a futuristic thing for other idiots!

But all of us who know Nick expect this. It is just his demeanor.

Over the years I have developed two theories about people. First of all, if my Labrador retriever's first impression of someone is positive, that speaks volumes about that individual's character. Secondly, if you really want to find out just what kind of person someone is, spend a week alone together in hunting camp. On both accounts, the Professor passed with flying colors.

There are so many things about Nick I could say. Like being with him when he shot his first mule deer buck with a longbow he made himself. Or the time we sat in a wall tent during a blizzard and got the tent so damn hot with the wood stove we ended up sitting around butt-naked drinking beer until late in the afternoon when we were surprised by some visitors who blasted into the tent. And there was the time we were hunting black bear on Kodiak Island and Nick had closed the distance between him and a feeding bear with a beautiful 300 yards stalk, only to fart so loud in a crouched position he scared the bear into the next valley. Or the time in 1990 when he and his wife helped me move my family from one state to another...on Christmas Eve...only to spend Christmas day with us in a rented house. That speaks volumes about the Professor's character.

Of course, we don't always hunt together, and in our aging years we seem to be a little more set in our ways. But in the end, I feel like the luckiest bowhunter in the world to have such a hunting partner as the Professor. Everybody should have such a friend.

Campfire Reflections ═══════════ **Twenty-one**

The Right Thing

As bowhunters, we are bound to a high standard of ethics both in and out of the field. Our concern for the hunted game animal cannot be anything but foremost in our mind when we step into the woods with our trusty weapon of choice. It is our responsibility to hunt as close as we can get, take only the best shots and strive for the perfect one-arrow, double lung shot to humanely bring down our quarry. However, sometimes fate takes a swipe at us and we must do whatever we can to make the right choice and to do the right thing. At times like this our decisions may be based on personal morals or other reasons.

No one takes bowhunting more seriously than I do. It is what I think about every waking hour of my life. I guess you might even say it is my job, but I do not wish to argue the ramifications of that statement, so let's just say for argument's sake it is my strongest hobby. As such I spend a lot of time in the field bowhunting with many different people in many different places. I've seen fate throw curves and watched as it has literally destroyed someone's self-confidence. This is bound to happen in any endeavor, but there are times when you have the opportunity to do the right thing.

Africa, 1996

I had spent six days in the African bush trying to find a respectable kudu. The hunting had been hard; water was everywhere and blinds by water holes were useless. I was spending the days stalking through the jungle with my guide Mika. There were many species I was interested in, but zebra was not one of them...then I saw one in the bush for the first time. They are without a doubt one of the most beautiful creatures to inhabit the African veldt. Right then and there I made a decision; I would spend my remaining time in Africa trying to stalk and shoot a zebra with my longbow.

To me there are a few plains game animals that say "Africa" when you see them for the first time. One of them is the giraffe, another the wildebeest, or gnu. But then there is the plains zebra, *Equus burchellii*. Theodore Roosevelt, in his excellent book *African Game Trails*, stated, "As a matter of fact the zebra's coloration is not protective at all; on the contrary it is exceedingly conspicuous..." when describing his opinions on the zebra's natural coloration. Since Roosevelt was hunting on the open plains in what are now known as Kenya and Uganda, I have to disagree somewhat with his opinion of the zebra. Although the zebra is indeed conspicuous in the open, with its white coat and black stripes it can literally disappear before your eyes in the bush. Their color schemes, along with their acute senses, have allowed this wonderful animal to thrive on the African veldt. Their dog-like barking is eerie the first time you hear it come to you from out of the darkness around a campfire at night, and the full crescent hoof marks they leave make you wonder how they can come and go without a sound.

Many ignorant individuals will state the zebra is nothing but a horse, but I know better. Their eyes, hearing and smell are second to none. They have all the reflexes of a whitetail and are twice as smart, and they can sense danger far better than any animal I have ever encountered. Ask anyone who has stalked a zebra and they'll tell you the same—the zebra is one of the hardest animals to hunt on the ground anywhere.

The next three days I spent working the bush with Mush Nichols, camp head and master Professional Hunter (PH) for Roger Whittall Safaris in Zimbabwe. We were working the Humani ranch trying to find zebra in huntable areas. What few stalks I was able to perform ended within a few hundred yards. Even with the cover I was not able to close within shooting distance.

Mush decided I should try another property on the eastern edge of Zimbabwe, so we loaded up the truck with gear and native trackers and drove the six hours there one afternoon. That evening we had dinner with the owners' son, walked through their luscious gardens, and made an honest attempt to put a dent in the wine cellar's top-notch collection of South African and Zimbabwean reds before turning in for the evening.

The next morning we were driving the ranch when we came across a herd of zebra feeding in the trees. I got out and made a stalk on them, but at 30 yards with the wind in my face they bolted away before I could get the shot I wanted. Two hours later I made another stalk on a herd feeding up the side of a rocky hill. As I made my way around the backside and crested the top, they were gone. We never saw them again.

After lunch we again found a small herd of four zebra feeding across an open swath of bush half way up a small hill and I got out to attempt another stalk. I told Mush to come back in two hours and I would meet him at the road. An hour and a half later, I finally crested the top of the hill where the zebra were feeding across. The wind was bucking and racing up the hill as I came over the top and took a stand behind a large rock. I couldn't hear anything because of the wind, so I nocked an arrow and peered around the boulder. Within a minute a large zebra stepped into view, broadside within 20 yards and put its head down to feed. The arrow was on its way toward the spot I had my eyes glued to, but the wind was working it down. The zebra jumped, my arrow flipped up, and I thought I had missed. The other three zebra ran up and the four of them walked over the hill.

I oozed up to the saddle where they had crossed and searched the area below me with binoculars, but could not see them. Looking down I saw a drop of crimson and knew I had a problem. Tracking back to the spot where the zebra had been when I took the shot, I followed what seemed to be a large amount of blood. I found my arrow in two pieces, with the broadhead end broken about four inches back and the feathered end covered with blood. But there was a three-inch section missing, presumably still in the zebra.

Mush and the trackers met me at the prescribed time and I told them of the ordeal. Mika and I tracked the zebra for about 300 yards over the hill and down into the trees while Mush took the truck around the hill. As Mika and I were following the spoor, a herd of zebra came running by us, spooked by a native carrying a bucket of water through the bush. They stopped within 75 yards of us, looking back at the native. Glassing the herd we could not determine if any of them was the one I had hit. Mush came down into the trees where we were and we discussed the situation. He decided we should take the truck up a hill to get a better vantage point to glass from. We knew the zebra was close, but we could not hope to find it by staying in the trees.

As we rounded a corner we came upon four zebra, a herd exactly like the one I had stalked. There were two yellow-tinted ones—a beautiful color caused from the animals rolling in the iron-rich soil—a young one and an old, very large one. The big zebra had to be the one I shot. We glassed them looking for any sign of blood or a wound, but after five minutes we couldn't be sure of anything. Then the old one turned away from us and I saw blood running down the inside of its front legs. Mush saw it at the same time and I grabbed my bow from Mika in the back of the truck...Mush grabbed his 30.06.

"I can stalk it and finish the job. We don't need the gun," I whispered to Mush. He was drawing a bead on the zebra as I spoke.

"T.J., you know the rules. If it is wounded, we must bring it down."

"I know that, but I want to do it my way, with the bow."

"If that zebra gets in with the larger herd, we will never find it before the wild dogs do. And you know what they will do to it. They will eat it alive," he said.

I felt sick. I had stalked this zebra on its own terms, waited for the best opportunity and had taken my best shot. (A later autopsy would show I had missed the heart by only two inches, the arrow entering the right leg, through the sternum and through the left leg.) But fate had its own idea of what was to happen and now I had a problem. Mush leveled the gun and I grabbed his arm. "Mush, I drew first blood. It is my problem, not yours. If we have to bring it down with the gun, then by God give me the gun and I'll finish what I started." Mush looked at me for a few seconds and handed over the Springfield. "What's it sighted in for?" I asked.

"One hundred and fifty yards," he replied.

I sat down and stared out over the savannah toward the four zebra. God, I wanted this to be different. Peering through the scope, I felt the familiar weight of the rifle. It had been some years since I trained with military weapons, but I knew the death for which I held in my hands. With a slight pull of my finger the zebra dropped to the ground. I rose, handed the gun to Mika in the back of the truck and turned to Mush. "That's why I don't hunt with a rifle," I said to him.

"Yes, T.J., I know, but it was the *right thing* to do, and you know it," Mush said.

He was right, and I knew it.

Idaho, 1996

We had spent the last eight days in Idaho's backcountry hunting elk. It was truly an elk hunt from hell. Besides the problems associated with using llamas to pack into the wilderness, the weather had tormented us every day of the hunt. Snow, sleet, hail, rain and high winds kept us in tents for most of the time. But we had managed to find the elk and I even missed a dandy bull one morning, but that is another story.

Now, as Nick and I soaked in a little-known hot spring along the Salmon River taking a much-needed bath, we sat staring the end of elk season in the face. Tomorrow would be the last day so we had to make the most of it. Our plans were to head into town and get a room, and then hunt an old familiar area that we knew held elk.

Early the next morning we were having coffee in the lodge when an older gentleman approached us. He introduced himself as Doc, and said that he had shot a bear late the night before and needed some help tracking it down. Nick and I finished our coffee and went with Doc in his rig to the last spot he had tracked the bear.

The spoor started out good and we made progress through the swamp the bear had entered. But two hours later it seemed the bear had given us the slip. Nick backtracked while I worked through a slough trying to pick up the trail. When we met back at the head of the swamp Nick had found the arrow and picked up the trail where the bear had doubled back on us. It had entered a large pile of willows and did not come out. Doc thanked us for the help and said he would get his friend to help him recover the bear. So the three of us headed back to Doc's truck and to the lodge for breakfast.

When we got back to the truck, Doc said he saw a mule deer lying down off the trail back in the swamp, that it didn't look too good. He asked if one of us wanted to shoot it. I looked at Nick and said, "You want to?" He just shook his head and handed me his longbow. "Hey, if it's sick we better go and see," I said.

Doc and I walked back down the trail toward where he had seen the deer. As we rounded a bend I saw a large mule deer doe lying down, facing away from us. Her head turned around as I neared and she stared at me. I had an arrow already nocked and I froze in my steps. She did-

She wasn't the buck I wanted, but her meat filled the freezer.

n't look too well. My mind wandered as to why she was lying there when all of a sudden she jumped straight up and burst out away from us. I saw she had a hole in her left side and I swung with her as she darted toward the marsh. The arrow caught her in the side and angled into her lungs as she made the brush.

"How did you get the shot off!" asked Doc. He was in total shock at how quick everything had happened. Come to think of it, so was I.

Nick came around the corner and I handed his bow back to him and asked him to help me pull the doe out of the marsh. We walked into the grass and found the deer within 20 feet of where I had hit her. Just below my arrow was a perfect three-blade cut of a broadhead, dead center in her paunch. From the looks of it she had been gut shot that morning by someone else and we had happened on to her.

When I had first approached the deer I didn't know whether or not I was going to shoot it. I didn't want to spend my only Idaho deer tag on a sick deer, but when she bolted and I saw the hole in her side my reflexes took over. It happened so fast I never even thought about it. If I had let her go she most likely would have died a horrible death, as a gut shot animal will never recover.

As I tagged the deer, I turned to Nick. "It was the right thing to do, Nick." He shook his head and I knew he understood why I took the shot.

So, what is the verdict on these two hunts? Should I be ashamed of my decisions in these two situations? Not a chance, and I'll tell you why. In the first instance I made a great stalk only to have a bad arrow. In the second I didn't really even hunt, however, I made a perfect shot and saved an animal from a hideous death.

Now I have one beautiful zebra rug from the Dark Continent for my office, which reminds me of the wonderful country and handsome people I met there, even though I can never claim it as a bow kill. It also taught me of the tenacity of African game, and it has done something else to me; I will have to return again and again to Africa—I must see more.

I also have a freezer of deer meat from the doe. I took it back to Nick's house and skinned it out, butchered it up and gave half to Nick, as is our custom when hunting together. There was some meat that had to be cast away, but other than that it was a fine eating animal, and I have the hide to adorn my office wall. Yes, I would have liked to have kept the deer tag until the late season when the big bucks come down from the mountains, but I was happy to take the deer under such circumstances.

Not everyone will agree with my opinions discussed here, and that is their business. But we can never forget that sometimes we may have to make decisions while hunting that may not always give us the outcome we are seeking. There are times when we must decide what is the *right thing* to do, for the animal and for bowhunting.

It is a decision only you can make. Make it wisely.

Twenty-two — *T.J. Conrads*

A Lost Valley

It has been said that to find yourself you must first find yourself lost. And even though I wasn't lost myself, the vast abyss that lie before me had not seen the encroachment of man...and very few of them at that. I felt as though I had stumbled into one of the last forgotten places smack dab in the middle of my home state of Idaho.

The sun had settled down behind the mountains to the west and the shadows oozed toward darkness. A crystal clear creek ran down through the valley floor snaking through vast, lush meadows of green grasses and wildflowers, interspersed with spruce, fir and pine. Up the far side of the canyon spruce, fir and aspen dotted the scenery, draping magnificently through the granite boulders and grassy meadows. A bald eagle soared on thermals above, eying me over as if I was some abstract being that had wandered into its living room. Come to think of it, I had done just that.

From deep within the dark timber, several hundred feet below my position on the side of the canyon, an elk ripped a bugle that reverberated throughout the valley. No sooner had the sound faded than two more bugles, from different parts of the valley, beckoned me. With a single sweep of my binoculars, I settled on an ivory tipped cervid of a size I had not seen in over 12 years of chasing these animals. In and out, through and around the meadows and trees, the bull moved his small harem of three cows and a calf.

It was dark now, too late to drop into the valley, so I sat and listened to the bulls bellow back and forth. Tomorrow would be another day, and I would have the opportunity to explore this isolated chunk of wilderness. I wandered back to camp, made a simple supper, and stared into the flames of the fire until the cold pushed me into my sleeping bag for the night.

There is a common misconception that we, as hunters, are losing numbers. The fallacy of this can be made readily apparent by accessing any state fish and game department license sales. The truth may be that we are becoming a smaller percentage as compared to actual population growth, but hunter numbers have increased...by my accounts much too high. The ATV, GPS, and other technological wonders have paved the way for a hunter to access what was once—and still should be—wilderness areas where woodsmanship and outdoor skills are necessary for one to enjoy. There seems to be an increasing number of hunters who are after the kill, and not the true experience of what bowhunting is all about.

It is because of this easy access that it becomes harder to find areas of wilderness where you can really enjoy a true wilderness experience, and a chance to hunt game that has seen few, if any, humans. Most of my treasured haunts that have given me many, many years of unfettered hunting are now littered with the tracks of boots, ATV ruts, and beer cans, the end result of this technological onslaught. To truly find a private area to hunt these days means getting off the beaten track, and that, for me, means loading up a backpack for a week excursion into unknown territory.

It was precisely this urge to get away from everyone that brought me to this place, a hard eight miles of hiking from the nearest road, away from any access trails for some idiot on a trail bike, or any other motorized vehicle for that matter. And what I found when I got here late in the day was indeed worth the effort. In the few short hours after I arrived, set up my one-man tent and scouted a few drainages, I had seen several elk, mule deer and grouse...and not another soul...not another boot print. It was paradise found at great effort, and the week ahead held promises of close encounters of the cervid kind.

Morning broke with several inches of snow on the ground and blizzard-like conditions. My camp was placed deep within a stand of heavy spruce on a ridge top to protect me from the winds. But even with the wall of spruce my tent was popping as the wind whistled through the trees. Not to worry: this tent had been through a 60 mile per hour hurricane in Alaska for two days and would hold through this. But my hunting opportunity seemed to be put on hold with near zero visibility and high winds.

The morning was spent cutting wood, building a lean-to for gear storage, and hanging a meat pole, something I thought I would need before the trip was over. Another pot of coffee, a late lunch of freeze-dried gruel, and then the snow stopped falling. Within a few minutes the sun broke through and I prepared to head out for an afternoon hunt.

It turned out to be a fabulous day with snow draped across the trees like angel hair, the spun fiberglass we used to lace through Christmas trees...until someone in a government office decided the stuff was too dangerous to be used around children. The rocky outcroppings glistened as the snow quickly melted in the bright sunshine. I managed to jump a few mulies and a covey or two of grouse, but no elk...no sign, no sound, nobody home.

On the hike back to camp I scored on several Angel Wing mushrooms, large, white delicacies that are often found on rotting aspens. These, I knew, would be a welcome addition to the freeze-dried beef and

peppers that were on the evening menu. After dinner I retired early to my sleeping bag. Just as I was about to fall asleep, off in the distance a wolf howled. His lonely, primeval voice echoed off the valley walls for several minutes before it stopped just as quickly as it had begun. It was all quiet again and I slowly nodded off.

There is a saying among Idahoans: if you don't like the weather, wait a few minutes and it will change. And change it did. A northern Chinook breathed down upon the valley and by the next morning the snow was all but a memory in my little neck of the woods. It was still brisk at dawn as I finished a small pot of coffee, loaded my hunting pack, and fell off the mountain, hoping to catch an elk in the meadows below.

For the next week I called elk, chased elk, and even managed to blow a few opportunities to kill elk, but still the meat pole remained empty, and I would have to hike out in two days due to other commitments. The next morning as I worked my way down into the valley for the last time I met up with a covey of young Ruffed grouse, five in all. In five shots I had three of them strapped to a leather thong hanging from my hunting pack. Young and tender, I now had secured a feast that would break the dull monotony of eating Mountain House meals three times a day for the last week or so.

Farther down the hill a lone male spruce grouse made the mistake of taking just a few seconds too long to walk away and was added to the now bursting larder.

In the bottom of the valley, among the luscious flora, elk spoor was everywhere. Trails were etched into the ground from years' of heavy use; it was as if I had managed to take a step back in time where game was plentiful and unmolested. In one meadow I found the complete skeleton of a huge 6x6 bull, dead for a year, its front right leg broken when it fell into a hole made from the creek running under the meadow. I thought about taking the antlers home, but I was two miles from camp, down in the bottom of a draw, and the rig was another eight miles beyond.

That was when it hit me; even though I had packed far enough back in where I was hunting virgin territory, it would be almost impossible to get an elk out in the day and a half I had left. With no help and limited time, I had to come to terms with the situation I found myself in.

A bugle wafted through the woods, then another much closer. Out of instinct, I dropped back into the shadows of some fir and bugled, nocking an arrow as I settled down into the brush.

It only took one call; the bull was there in front of me within seconds, bugling for all his worth. Six tines per side, he was picture perfect. This was my chance to finally arrow a big bull elk, something that I have never been able to accomplish in all the years I have chased them. Not finding the aggressor, the bull turned to leave and as he presented the quartering away target, I drew my bow. He kept walking and soon was out of range and bugling as he fell down the hill. The tension on the bowstring slowly eased as I let down and I just sat there, trying to justify why I failed to shoot.

I sat in the fleeting light listening to several bulls bugle throughout the valley, the vision of that magnificent animal wafting through my mind. It was now dark. My hunt was over. Grouse were on the menu for dinner so I loaded my hunting pack and made my way back to camp in the dark. Tomorrow would bring a long, lonely hike out to civilization.

Several years have passed since that hunt took place. I have had lots of time to think about why I let that bull go and no matter how much I try to rationalize my actions, I feel I did the right thing. That dude was toast. All I had to do was drop the string. But I had run out of time. I needed to be out by the following sunset. In my desire to get as far away from other hunters, I had placed myself in a situation where I knew had I killed that bull, I would not have been able do it justice. And in the end, I learned a little about myself, that I had finally reached a point in my bowhunting career where the experience of the chase outweighs the trophy.

I had found a place where the elk roam free, where few, if any hunters ever reach. Pack animals may be the answer, but I have had my dealings with such beasts—horses, llamas and goats—and in the end have opted to do without their ornery attitudes and high maintenance. I prefer to be self-contained, taking everything I need on my back. But the years are adding up; the mountains get a little steeper each season and my body is telling me my days of backpack hunting are numbered. Life must go on, but I find it hard to come to terms with my own mortality. Each year seems a little shorter, and I find I want to hunt harder.

And so it goes....

I often think about that secluded valley and all the experiences and sensations I felt and had there. The topo maps of the area show all the notations of springs, grouse kills, elk wallows and encounters with wapiti. And I often think of going back, to experience once again the feeling of being alone, of seeing raw, untouched wilderness, and no other hunters; a chance to go and get lost again, and then to find myself once more...to feel once again the loneliness and pure experience of a place left untouched by man. After all, that is what hunting is really about in the end.

Twenty-three ══════════════════ *T.J. Conrads*

Remembering Monty

I was going through some old files one day when I came across a folder containing several letters in it. Many were from friends and acquaintances over the years; others kept for legal purposes. One, however, from Monarch Longbows, made me stop and reminisce. It was a letter from a good friend of mine, long dead now, Monty Moravec. With a little hesitation and some deep thought, I slipped the weathered paper from its envelope and began to read the words hand-written across the pages.

The beginning of the letter said it all: "I guess a little of your talent rubbed off on me at the Longbow Safari in Canada this past year. This is my biggest bull and black bear yet." I glanced at one of the images of a large 6-point bull elk, Monty smiling broadly from deep within the Montana wilderness. The other showed a large black bear and Monty, straining to hold the exceptionally large head up.

Hell, I thought, I don't have that kind of talent, much less luck. I stared at the images of huge animals and one of my good friends. I could hear his voice and see his quirky little smile as I read the letter. Then I sat back to pull out all the best—and some of the worst—memories I had of this strapping young man, a man who left this world much too soon.

I first met Monty in July, 1989 at the North America Longbow Safari in Golden, British Columbia. In addition to his fuel servicing business, he was working for Byron Schurg, who owned Monarch Longbows out of Missoula, Montana, at the time and was shooting a massive 75# longbow he had made under Byron's guidance. We hit it off right away shooting longbows and sharing campfires with other longbow enthusiasts and made plans to hunt together the following fall.

We spent the next few years hunting whitetails in the fall and sharing other hunting experiences. He was a great friend, fun to be around, and always getting us into strange predicaments.

At the Traditional Bowhunters Exposition in Hastings, Michigan, in January 1992, Monty asked me if I would like to come and hunt black bear with him in northern Idaho that spring. I agreed, and ordered a custom tulipwood longbow from him at the same time. I figured I needed a new bow, and what better way to break it in than on a hunt with the bowyer who made it for me?

I arrived in Missoula that May and we traveled over the border into Idaho where Monty had already set up camp and had a few working baits. There were other friends of Monty's there, as well as Byron Schurg, who had sold Monarch Longbows to Monty.

That first night, after we had returned from an evening hunt, Byron and the others had a huge campfire going so Monty and I joined in the camaraderie.

"You like gin and tonic, don't you?" Monty asked me. A rather dumb question, if you know me at all!

"Of course, I would love one, " I replied. He pulled out a fifth of Tanqueray and poured two drinks: one for him and one for me, in very large glasses.

The last thing I remember of the evening was Monty and I crawling back to his tent. I awoke with the worst hangover I have ever had, as well as having the strong desire to relieve my swollen bladder. Naked and not feeling well, I rolled out of the wall to meet several of the other campers sitting around. Not batting an eye, I stumbled through the group, across the dirt road, and relieved myself before stumbling back through several horrified people.

When I entered the tent, there was Monty, laughing uncontrollably with his video recorder on. "I got the whole thing! From the time you woke up to now!" He said. I looked at the table between our cots. The gin bottle was empty. He made exactly two drinks with one fifth.

We hunted hard all week, sitting in treestands over bait, stalking bears in the woods, and finally doing a honey burn on the evening before I had to fly back to Seattle. We had set two treestands next to each other but on different trees so he could film me. With a Coleman Peak 1 stove burning, a 1-pound coffee can with about two inches of honey was placed inside a crib made of pine logs. Now it was just a waiting game.

We sat there as the honey spitted, spat and finally caught fire. I was just about to bale out of the tree when the fire subdued and the fuel ran out of the stove. Not five minutes later, a bear appeared well below us. Then another slightly larger bear came walking in from directly in front of us.

"Too small," I whispered toward Monty.

"That's a big bear, T.J.," Monty said back to me.

It was my last night, and I had seen some huge bears, one of them we got on film that was twice the size of this one. When the bear walked over to the logs and dipped his head into them, I went on autopilot and let fly. At the release the bear reared up and the arrow took him in the spine. The roar was defending as the bear zipped down the mountain, dragging its hind legs.

"Terrible penetration," I said.

"I think you spined him," Monty whispered back.

We sat there until dark and went back to camp. It was a long night and when the sun finally appeared we had all my gear loaded in Monty's truck and were headed up to find the bear.

It was easy to follow the trail—a large swath of knocked down plants, trees and grass descended almost 600 yards straight down the mountain into a box canyon of cedar and pine. At the creek, which was rushing heavily, the grass was matted down where the bear had laid down. All of sudden Monty looked up and said, "There he is! He's coming for us!"

I glanced up and saw the bear not 20 yards away on the other side of the creek, growling and rising up. The next thing I saw was an orange shaft take him square through the chest as he folded into the grass.

"T.J., that was the finest shot I have ever seen!" Monty said to me. I was impressed as well, as the first arrow was something less than perfect.

Pictures, skinning and boning complete, we packed the bear up the hill after finding a log on which to cross the roaring creek. I made it to the airport with less than 30 minutes to spare. As I walked into the gangway, I turned and Monty was standing on the other side of the glass wall, smiling back at me.

A week later I received a phone call from Noelle, Monty's girlfriend, asking how I felt. I told her I felt fine, and then she told me Monty was in the hospital, fighting for his life with viral encephalitis.

Apparently, sometime on our bear hunt either a mosquito or a rodent bit Monty, transferring the virus to him. After I had flown home, nobody saw or heard from Monty for three days. Finally, Byron Schurg went over to Monty's house and found him incapacitated in bed. A trip to the emergency room and the virus was discovered, a virus that causes the brain to swell resulting in damaged brain cells and death. Since there is no cure for a virus, the doctors at the hospital had to treat the symptoms.

I got a call from Monty about six days after he was admitted and we talked briefly before the nurse made him hang up the phone and get some rest. He sounded tired, but was in good spirits and was only worried about me. After nine days in the hospital, he was released. Little did I know that this viral bout would change Monty forever.

That winter we hunted whitetails in Montana in sub-freezing weather out of Lincoln. He didn't really seem the same as before, but I just figured it was residual trauma from the virus. Although we didn't kill a deer, we had a blast.

The following spring we again headed back to northern Idaho for a bear hunt, but this time we rented a cabin at the Lochsa Lodge on the Lochsa River. The owners, Gus and Gerri, made us a special deal, as they always did for Monty. In their lodge were several pictures of Monty in his kayak from many years earlier when he pioneered the Selway and Lochsa Rivers for kayaking. He was the first to do all the northern rivers alone in a kayak, and the photos of him in the lodge were of legend proportion; every new river runner had Monty to thank, and Gus and Gerri made sure everyone knew it.

The hunting was lousy so we spent much of the time looking at property to buy along the river and spending time in the cabin talking. Unknown to me until then, Monty had lost his sense of smell and taste after the bout with the virus the year before, and eating was just something he had to do. He always complained that the only thing he could smell was the odor of electrical insulation burning. He also suffered from constant headaches that made him irritable and hard to be around.

One evening some of the young kayakers who knew Monty came to our cabin and invited us to a party they were having up at an old slash camp. Always one for adventure, Monty agreed and we drove up later that evening. When we pulled into their camp there, right in front of us on a flatbed truck with another truck's lights illuminated it, were two strippers...in the middle of the wilderness, of all places!

I went off to talk to some of the kayakers I knew and grab a beer while Monty grabbed his wallet and walked over to the flatbed. When I returned, there was Monty, a dollar bill rolled up and placed in each of his ears, and two more stuck in his nostrils, and he was lying on the truck bed with a smile on his face. That image of Monty is forever burned into my mind, and I smile every time I think of it.

That summer I was attending the Great Lakes Longbow Invitational in Brighton, Michigan. Monty had flown back with several dozen bows and had rented a van. Every night when the dealer tents would shut down we would head over to this old restaurant called The Log Cabin. Two old Greek cousins ran it and their special—every night—was a 24 ounce marinated porterhouse steak with all the fried potatoes and Greek salad you could eat, all for only $16.00.

One evening after dinner we were heading into town for a drink

Campfire Reflections 173

On his third solo float trip down the Moose John, Monty took this magnificent bull.

and to visit with some friends when a possum ran across the road in front of the van.

"Go catch it, T.J.!" Monty yelled as he slammed on the brakes. I dove out of the van, not even thinking about what I was doing, ran after the possum as Monty turned the van's lights into the woods, and grabbed that critter's tail. I mean to tell you, that thing was like a gyro in my hand, turning, spitting and growling as I ran back to the van and tossed it inside. Everybody flew out of the van except Monty, who was laughing his head off. "I didn't think you'd do it!" He said. It took a few minutes, but we finally got the possum out of the van and off we went to town. Things like this happened all the time with Monty. He just loved to play jokes and kid with people.

It was some time in July, 1995, and I was packing up for a business trip to Oklahoma City and thought I would call Monty and see how he was doing. He would call at least once a month, usually every other week, and we'd talk for over an hour. He loved to stay in touch with his friends, and we enjoyed each other's company so much that expensive phone bills were part of the relationship.

But this evening he was quiet and short, and did not want to talk.

"How's it going?" I said.

"OK," was his response.

"What are you doing this evening? Anything exciting?" I asked.

"Building bows," he replied; short, curt, and to the point...not like Monty at all.

I assumed he was having a fight with his new girlfriend, Barb, since I could hear her in the background, so I told him I was leaving for three weeks and he could reach me at my apartment in Oklahoma City. All he said was, "Bye."

The next day was long as I flew from Seattle to Denver and on to Oklahoma City and when I checked into my apartment there were six messages waiting for me. One was from my wife, who said that Monty had passed away the night before. I was stunned. I had just talked with him...what could have been so bad that would have caused him to die? The next message was from Rich Unger of R & J Enterprises with the same message. In fact, each and every message was the same...and then the last one was from my good friend Jay Massey.

"T.J., I didn't want you to hear this from me, but you need to call me. Monty committed suicide last night."

I was devastated, and just sat there for half an hour before I could even call Jay back. The sense of fear, loneliness and loss were just too much for me.

What I was later to find out, which was verified to me by the Ravalli County Coroner in a telephone call three weeks later, was that some time after Monty and I had hung up, his girlfriend left for an out of state trip, and he proceeded to his bedroom where he placed a shotgun to his forehead and pulled the trigger.

No note. No goodbye, no kiss my ass...no nothing. He left the party and never told anyone why. Oh, there were lots of conspiracy stories: he was murdered (the Coroner proved that false), he was robbed, he had money problems...all the normal denial reasons, of which I had several myself. I, nor just about everyone I knew, had an answer, and we never will.

Monty's family had him cremated, his ashes deposited some place where I do not know. Monarch Longbows was sold to Monty's good friend and bowyer Chris Landstrom, who stills builds them today.

The tulipwood longbow Monty made for me sits in my home office.

I know I should take it out and hunt with it again, and maybe someday I will. But for now, it is one of the few reminders of my friend—the laughs, good times, hunts and other not so telling things he was known for. And the bear I shot with him at my side resides in a place of honor in my living room, saved in a life-size mount, which reminds me of our great hunt, and the ultimate devastation that resulted in the loss of one of traditional archery's great guys.

I was hunting mountain goats in October of 1995 in central Washington. It had been a hard two weeks being alone when I finally killed a goat. The first thing I thought of was to call Monty. He always knew how this unique animal held a special place in my life. But it had been several months since he had died.

I was sitting in camp, looking at the goat horns, when a blue grouse lit into a tamarack tree behind me. I quickly brought the bird to bag, then started a fire and roasted it. All I thought about that evening was how much fresh roasted grouse meant to Monty. I hoped he was watching me as I savored every last bite of that wonderful meal.

It has been a decade since Monty died, and the pain and sense of loss are still with me. I often wonder what I could have done that night so long ago, if I had only known, to prevent such a terrible tragedy to such a young and wonderful man, my friend. If I had only known...I could have flown over right away...I should have kept him on the phone...There are so many things that I just don't know.

"The disease killed him, Tim," Noelle has repeatedly told me. "He was gone the day he came out of the hospital, and there is nothing you, nor anyone else, could have done. Quit beating yourself up over it. You were his best friend, and yet you never saw it coming either."

I think of Monty often, and look at what few pictures I still have of him with his Dall sheep, moose, bear, elk and several huge whitetails. But two pictures I hold dear exist on my home office corkboard. One is of Monty in a kayak, on the Lochsa River, doing what he loved to do best next to bowhunting. The other is a black and white photo of Monty holding a deer mouse that he had baited with bread and shot with his bow one night while we were hunting bear, his grin as wide as can be.

There are so many stories I remember about my friend, like the

Monty on the Middle Fork of the Salmon River in Idaho. He was one of the finest whitewater kayakers I ever knew.

time he created a one-tree forest fire while trying to do a honey burn, and ended up bailing out of the stand at 15 feet. Or the time he walked out of our cabin as I was asleep, and returned with a blow-up doll that he placed in bed with me and took pictures, then threatened to use as blackmail if I didn't get up and have a beer with him: it was two in the morning and he couldn't sleep. He wanted to talk about hunting, girls and what we should do in the future when we got too old to crawl around in the hills. Or the time he was on his second of three solo raft hunts down the Moose John River in Alaska when his pepper spray accidentally went off in his pants while fishing. He spent the next several hours sitting in the river, unable to stand up because of the burning. It wasn't funny at the time, but he and I laughed about that for many, many years. He was just such a joy to spend time with.

Once a year I pull out two of his videos he made for me, make a drink, and sit alone in my den and place them in the VCR. One is of our bear hunt in 1992 when he contracted the viral encephalitis. The other is a series of vignettes of a year in the life of Monty the bowhunter, from early season bear and deer hunts, to out of state hunts, a 9-day backpack hunt for elk, to finally treeing a lion in December only to break his bowstring and let the cat go.

But the one thing that always stays with me was where in the video, after he has taken a few grouse, and he says, "There's nothing like the taste of fresh grouse roasted over an open fire." That was my friend.

Tonight I am sitting around a campfire, on a ridge somewhere in central Idaho, scratching out these words about my friend into my notebook. I stalked two bull elk this evening without getting a shot, but managed to slip a Zwickey through a blue grouse, which has been roasting in the Dutch oven with several Angel Wing mushrooms I picked from a rotting aspen stump down in the valley below. The oven is removed from the coals and allowed to rest before being opened. I make a drink, stoke the campfire with another pitch log, and settle down to eat alone in the darkness. The wind has picked up and the temperature is dropping...a front is moving in. I zip up my wool coat and sit back to enjoy a meal—alone, as usual—taken from the mountain.

As I stare into the flickering flames, I think back on all the good folks I have met and had the rare pleasure to share a campfire with along life's strange trails, many of who are no longer with us.

And I remember Monty.